I0829400

This diary belongs to

____

____

HERTFORDSHIRE PRESS (UK)
In conjunction with
the Eurasian Creative Guild
https://www.1.eurasiancreativeguild.uk/
First published by Hertfordshire Press 2021

VOICES OF FRIENDS
POETRY ALMANAC 2021
Original poems ©

Translators Alina Moiseykina, Anatoly Lobov, Elena Aslanyan, Elena Bosler-Guseva, Irina Petrova, John Farndon, Marina Podlesnaya, Mikhail Ananov, Rashid Yugaziev, Sagyn Berkinalieva, Sergey Mainagashev (Tom Sidbay), Tatiana Vasilieva,
Project manager Angelina Kransnogir
English Editor John Farndon

A CIP catalogue record for this book is available in the British Library

ISBN 978-1-913356-24-8

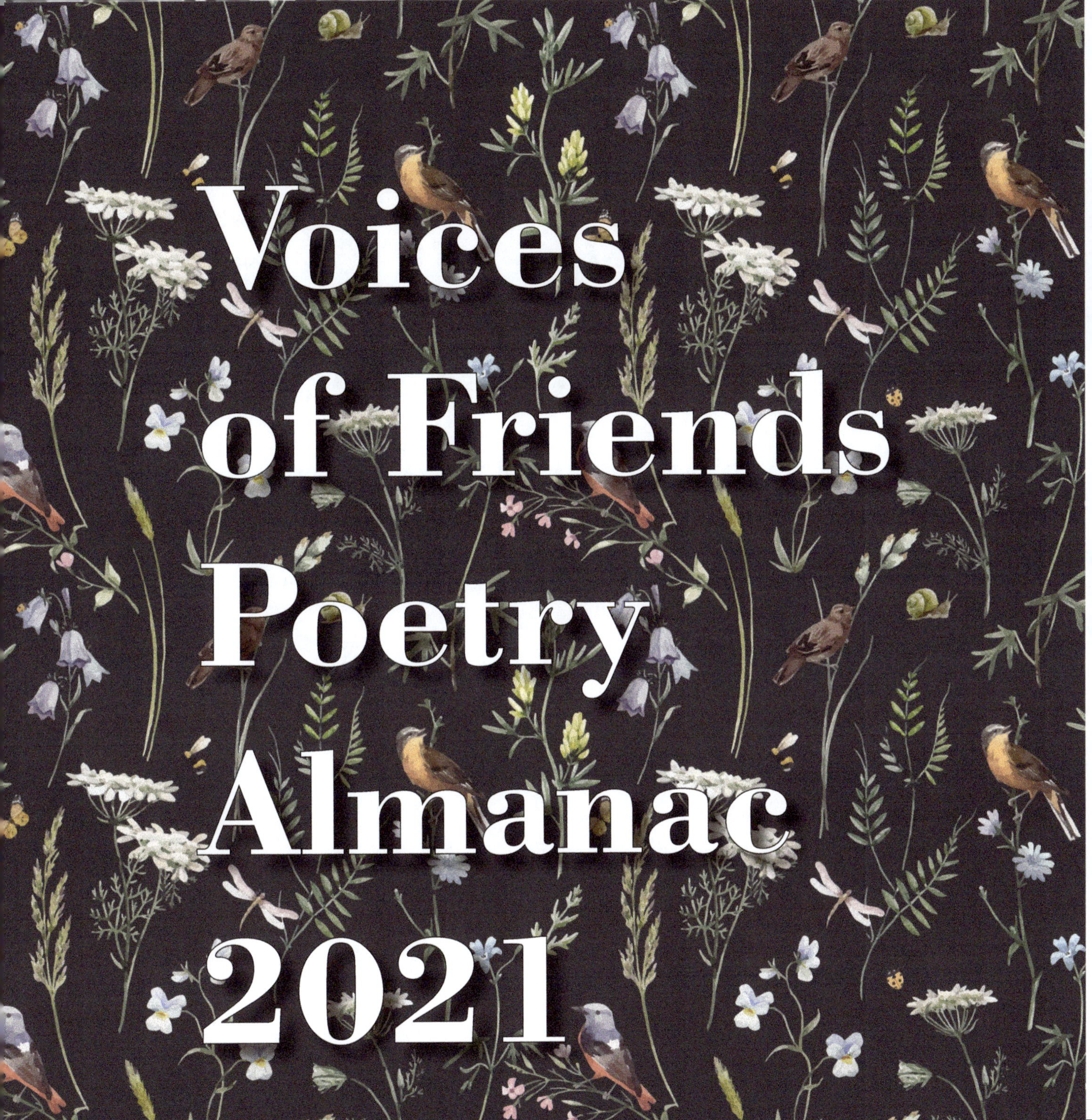
Voices
of Friends
Poetry
Almanac
2021

INTRODUCTION BY JOHN FARNDON

Welcome to our circle of poetry and friendship!

Poetry is so deeply embedded in the human soul that it seems to be part of every culture, and it communicates at a deep level beyond nations, beyond ethnicity and has the power to make us laugh, to make us cry, to feel outrage, to feel love – to feel our deep human connection. It brings us together in a very special way.

That's why we decided to put together this unique book of poetry that crosses boundaries, to create a bond of poetry across Eurasia. This is a truly international collection, bringing together poems from poets of many different nationalities and eras. Some are as they were written in their original language, whether it is Armenian or Italian, Spanish or Kyrgyz. But most are also translated into English or Russian, so that as many people as possible may read them as possible.

One of the special things about this collection is that it is not one person's personal choice; it is a unique collaboration. Poets from all over Eurasia were invited to submit their own work, and readers could submit their own choice of classic poets. The result is an astonishingly rich variety of work. Each poem is a gift, from one country to another, one friend to another, a joint mixtape of poetry. That's why the subtitle is 'Voices of Friends.'

My task as editor, then, was not to choose the poems to include in any way. That was done already by each and every contributor. This creates some extraordinary and arresting juxtapositions, between a time-tested masterpiece and a new unknown piece from an unfamiliar language.

Yes, there are famous and much loved poets in here – Shakespeare, Pushkin, Lermontov, Abai, Lorca, Petrarch and many more. But there are also poets being seen in print for the first time.

We've called it an Almanac because the collection is organized by the calendar. The idea is for these poems to take you through the year. And so every week there are two different poets, sometimes more, and some poets appear several times during the year.

It's arranged in date order, but there is absolutely no compulsion to read it that order, following it like a diary. You can do that of course, and that might be a delightful approach. But we also invite you to treat this as a box of chocolates, for you to dip and take your pick wherever takes your fancy.

You will encounter one poet many times throughout the book and that is the Scottish poet Sir Walter Scott. 2021 is the 250th anniversary of Scott's birth, and this book is in part a celebration of that anniversary. Today, Scott is best known as the pioneering author of historical novels, such as Ivanhoe, but he first made a name for himself as a poet. Indeed, he was the most widely read, most acclaimed poet of the Romantic age, combining the rough energy of traditional ballads with a contemporary mastery of language and form. Byron admired him greatly and through him his influence can be seen in the verse of Pushkln and Lermontov and many more.

Scott's poetry has been eclipsed today by his own much-loved novels, and by other poets. But we felt it deserved a new showcase. It would be interesting to try and spot the influence in some of our other poets across our wide-ranging collection, but I'll leave that to the scholars.

A word about the English versions of these poems and their translations. Some poems were submitted already translated by the poets themselves, and I've made minimal changes with these, because they are the poet's choice. Many, however, were submitted in the original language and given an initial translation by bilingual translators including Alina Moseykina and Tatiana Vasilieva. I have then modified these translations so that they work as English verse as close as possible to the original.

2020 has been a bad year all around the world for many, many people – not just the pandemic, but war, political oppression and suppression, poverty, homelessness, famine, dreadful weather and much more. No wonder people can't wait for it to be over. Well, we're nearly there.

Scott would have known the feeling. 1831, when Scott was 60, was a 2020=like year in Scotland, too, with a cholera epidemic forcing everyone into quarantine, and persuading people there was a conspiracy afoot. Sound familiar? The conspiracy was that doctors were killing off their cholera patients to provide cadavers for medical schools, just as the infamous Edinburgh murderers Burke and Hare had two years earlier. Fellow Scots poet James Hogg, known as the Ettrick Shepherd, wrote scathingly and very wittily about how glad he would be to see the back of this terrible year, with deliberately silly rhymes for cholera, and 'burking' to describe the conspiracies.

The poem begins like this:

> "O Eighteen hundred thirty one
> Thou hast been an intolera-
> Ble year for fume, for fudge, and flame
> For Burking and for cholera."

And ends like this:

> "Farewell, farewell! God speed thy flight
> Far o'er the regions polar a
> Long farewell to thee—jade outright
> Thy burking, bill, and cholera."

Many of us wish the same good riddance to 2020, and so this Almanac and its rich and varied basket of poetry is our gift to a wonderful new year, 2021.

Happy New Year to you!

But before I let you go, I would just like to express my sincere thanks to the many people involved in this project. Firstly, there's all the rich community of Eurasian Creative Guild, without who this wouldn't have been possible, and everyone who has submitted poems. Secondly, I would like to thank Marat Ahmedjanov, and Angelina Krasnogir for all their amazing inspiration and hard work in bringing this together. And thirdly and most of all, I would like to thank all the poets, dead and alive, who have given us the gift of their words.

Come and join us, friends, in our poetic year!

John Farndon

London, 16th December 2020

CALENDAR 2021

JANUARY

M	T	W	T	F	S	S
				1	2	3
4	5	6	7	8	9	10
11	12	13	14	15	16	17
18	19	20	21	22	23	24
25	26	27	28	29	30	31

FEBRUARY

M	T	W	T	F	S	S
1	2	3	4	5	6	7
8	9	10	11	12	13	14
15	16	17	18	19	20	21
22	23	24	25	26	27	28

MARCH

M	T	W	T	F	S	S
1	2	3	4	5	6	7
8	9	10	11	12	13	14
15	16	17	18	19	20	21
22	23	24	25	26	27	28
29	30	31				

APRIL

M	T	W	T	F	S	S
			1	2	3	4
5	6	7	8	9	10	11
12	13	14	15	16	17	18
19	20	21	22	23	24	25
26	27	28	29	30		

MAY

M	T	W	T	F	S	S
					1	2
3	4	5	6	7	8	9
10	11	12	13	14	15	16
17	18	19	20	21	22	23
24	25	26	27	28	29	30
31						

JUNE

M	T	W	T	F	S	S
	1	2	3	4	5	6
7	8	9	10	11	12	13
14	15	16	17	18	19	20
21	22	23	24	25	26	27
28	29	30				

JULY

M	T	W	T	F	S	S
			1	2	3	4
5	6	7	8	9	10	11
12	13	14	15	16	17	18
19	20	21	22	23	24	25
26	27	28	29	30	31	

AUGUST

M	T	W	T	F	S	S
						1
2	3	4	5	6	7	8
9	10	11	12	13	14	15
16	17	18	19	20	21	22
23	24	25	26	27	28	29
30	31					

SEPTEMBER

M	T	W	T	F	S	S
	1	2	3	4	5	
6	7	8	9	10	11	12
13	14	15	16	17	18	19
20	21	22	23	24	25	26
27	28	29	30			

OCTOBER

M	T	W	T	F	S	S
				1	2	3
4	5	6	7	8	9	10	11
12	13	14	15	16	17	18
19	20	21	22	23	24	25
26	27	28	29	30	31	

NOVEMBER

M	T	W	T	F	S	S
1	2	3	4	5	6	7
8	9	10	11	12	13	14
15	16	17	18	19	20	21
22	23	24	25	26	27	28
29	30					

DECEMBER

M	T	W	T	F	S	S
		1	2	3	4	5
6	7	8	9	10	11	12
13	14	15	16	17	18	19
20	21	22	23	24	25	26
27	28	29	30	31		

BAYANGALI ALIMZHANOV (KAZAKHSTAN)

World full of mysteries

Don't rage so much at life, my friend –
If you give up, how can it ever mend?
And don't give in to grief so much –
You could lose all faith in the end.

Open your heart's palace for a while –
What's the worst can happen if you smile?
Just be careful not to laugh too much
Or buffoonery will become your style.

There's no need to head each beck and call.
No need to bow and scrape to all –
Bend all the time like this and you
Could end a humpback, half as tall.

And don't puff out your chest too far –
Or when you lie down it'll look bizarre.
Don't let a froth of lies go to your head –
The bubbles will burst and leave a scar.

Don't fritter your energy. Don't go on and on.
What will you do when it's all gone?
And don't let go to all restraint –
You'll be a habitual sinner before you're done.

Don't waste time admiring your lovely face –
What happens when sickness takes its place?
And don't fawn and pander to everyone
Or your true love will sink without a trace.

01
JANUARY

If you swap your beating heart for gold
What can sustain you when you're old?
Just believe in yourself sincerely
And you'll survive all setbacks, I am told.

I don't say it will be a breeze,
Nor that every meal will please.
Life offers you both pain and joy
And the richest feast of mysteries!

Have you got a friend?

A man complains he has no friend
But is a lack of friendship really the end?
Can't drifting clouds and spring birds be enough?
Can't the great world of life be your friend?

True friendship is a gift of the land.
And though its winds aren't yours to command
And yet, the land's your friend – do you understand?
So ask yourself, in the end,
Have you truly offered it your hand?

So do not weep when you feel alone;
If you're by yourself, the fault's your own!
If you cannot give your heart to the land,
Then you'll never see the love it's shown.

Like wandering clouds

Like wandering clouds, your soul drifts on,
But all too fast your past is gone!
Where now's that boy by the apple tree
Who looked for the sky to dance upon?

Like those brave riders from days gone by,
We all still in our childhood saddles lie.
'Where are you going, and what's ahead?'
We ask the clouds blown through the sky.

Sometimes we weep like falling rain –
Our tears a drizzling mist again.
Or is the secret truth that we
Behave as clouds, or is that vain?

There's sureness in the infinite blue,
Yet the caravans of clouds scoot through.
A cloudless sky is blank and sad –
Clouds' shapes paint the sky for you.
As they float off over the horizon,
They bear your greetings with them too.

徐志摩

我独坐在半山的石上，
看前峰的白云蒸腾，
一只不知名的小雀，
嘲讽着我迷惘的神魂。

白云一饼饼的飞升，
化入了辽远的无垠；
但在我逼仄的心头，啊，
却凝敛着惨雾与愁云！

皎洁的晨光已经透露，
洗净了青屿似的前峰；
像墓墟间的燐光惨淡，
一星的微焰在我的胸中。

但这惨淡的弱火一星，
照射着残骸与余烬，
虽则是往迹的嘲讽，
却绵绵的长随时间进行！

A FAINT FLASH OF FIRE

I'm sitting alone on a mountain slope,
Watching a white fog rise from other peaks,
An unknown little bird is taunting me,
Taunting my misty baffled soul.

One by one white clouds are rising high up,
Interflowing in a vastness of skies,
Oh, my cramped little heart, again you're left
Covered in gloomy clouds of misery!

Rays of a rising sun have broken through,
Sharpening blue shapes of island-like peaks;
Like a dim light that glows among the graves
Is a tiny spark of a flame in my heart.

This dim glow, this faint flash of fire
Sheds light on ruins and ashes left by defeat,
Even though the past can mock and belittle,
Don't stop following the pace of time!

03
JANUARY

28 MONDAY

29 TUESDAY

30 WEDNESDAY

31 THURSDAY

01 FRIDAY

02 SATURDAY

03 SUNDAY

HARP OF THE NORTH, FAREWELL!
(The Lady of the Lake, Canto VI)

Harp of the North, farewell! The hills grow dark,
On purple peaks a deeper shade descending;
In twilight copse the glow-worm lights her spark,
The deer, half-seen, are to the covert wending.
Resume thy wizard elm! the fountain lending,
And the wild breeze, thy wilder minstrelsy;
Thy numbers sweet with nature's vespers blending,
With distant echo from the fold and lea,
And herd-boy's evening pipe, and hum of housing bee.

Yet, once again, farewell, thou Minstrel Harp!
Yet, once again, forgive my feeble sway,
And little reck I of the censure sharp
May idly cavil at an idle lay.
Much have I owed thy strains on life's long way,
Through secret woes the world has never known,
When on the weary night dawned wearier day,
And bitterer was the grief devoured alone.—
That I o'erlive such woes, Enchantress! is thine own.

Hark! as my lingering footsteps slow retire,
Some spirit of the Air has waked thy string!
'Tis now a seraph bold, with touch of fire,
'Tis now the brush of Fairy's frolic wing.
Receding now, the dying numbers ring
Fainter and fainter down the rugged dell;
And now the mountain breezes scarcely bring
A wandering witch-note of the distant spell—
And now, 'tis silent all!—Enchantress, fare thee well!

04
JANUARY

FARVÄL, DU NORDENS HARPA!
(Sjöfröken) Sjette Sången

Farväl, du nordens harpa! Natten sänder
På fjellens purpurspetsar skuggor ner;
I dunkel lund en lysmask gnistan tänder
Och jag till hidet hjorten smyga ser.
Vid källans brädd skall vinden i dig susa;
På almens gren jag åter hänger dig.
Der må du i naturens samklang tjusa
Och dina ljud med toner blanda sig
Af bin som surra, vattenfall som brusa.

Ännu en gång: farväl du sångarharpa!
Ännu en gång: förlåt mitt svaga spel!
Hvad bryr det mig om granskarns synglas skarpa
I mina sånger leta efter fel?
Jag lärt af dig att glömma oförrätter,
I sorgens mörker hoppets ljus du tändt;
Du var min tröst på lifvets ödeslätter,
I hemligt qval, hvars grund ej verlden känt,
Då hemska dagar följt förgråtna nätter. —

Hör! Luftens ande nu i harpan klingar,
Då långsamt jag från källan återgår.
Jag suset hör af Alfers lätta vingar;
Och nu en Sylf så muntert strängen slår!…
Så småningom de milda ljud försvinna,
Jag skiljes då från sångens gudaslägt?…
Som brutna suckar de mitt öra hinna,
Svagt hviskade af vindens svala flägt. —
Nu är allt tyst! — Farväl förtjusarinna!

*Translation
by Lars Arnell (1829)*

Frost and Sun

Frost and sun – what a glorious day!
Yet still, sweet friend, you sleep away –
It's time, gorgeous, for you to stir:
Open wide your dreamy eyes
To catch the dawnglow in northern skies –
Rise up like a northern star!

Last night, remember, a blizzard seethed.
In sombre skies, the thick clouds heaved.
The moon, a livid blotch, struck shadows
Through the dark and churning brume,
While you sat miserably in the gloom –
Well now... look out through the windows!

Under vivid azure skies
A luxurious pure carpet lies –
Snow, sparkling in the brilliant light.
Bare trees present their blackening sheen;
Through the white, spruce growing green;
Beneath the ice, a river glistening bright.

Our room is filled with an amber glow
And now the kindling's on the go,
Crackling merrily on the stove inside –
How nice to sit by its warmth all day!
But hey...why not order out the sleigh
With the chestnut mare and ride?

Swishing over the snow we'll race.
Surrender, sweet friend, to the pace
As our urgent steed pulls fast!
We'll shoot through lonely fields and thence
Through thickets so recently too dense...
To my beloved riverbank, at last.

04 MONDAY

05 TUESDAY

06 WEDNESDAY

07 THURSDAY

08 FRIDAY

09 SATURDAY

10 SUNDAY

THE CRUSADER'S RETURN (Ivanhoe)

High deeds achieved of knightly fame,
From Palestine the champion came;
The cross upon his shoulders borne,
Battle and blast had dimm'd and torn.
Each dint upon his batter'd shield
Was token of a foughten field;
And thus, beneath his lady's bower,
He sung as fell the twilight hour:—

"Joy to the fair!—thy knight behold,
Return'd from yonder land of gold;
No wealth he brings, nor wealth can need,
Save his good arms and battle-steed
His spurs, to dash against a foe,
His lance and sword to lay him low;
Such all the trophies of his toil,
Such—and the hope of Tekla's smile!

"Joy to the fair! whose constant knight
Her favour fired to feats of might;
Unnoted shall she not remain,
Where meet the bright and noble train;
Minstrel shall sing and herald tell—
'Mark yonder maid of beauty well,
'Tis she for whose bright eyes were won
The listed field at Askalon!

"'Note well her smile!—it edged the blade
Which fifty wives to widows made,
When, vain his strength and Mahound's spell,
Iconium's turban'd Soldan fell.
Seest thou her locks, whose sunny glow
Half shows, half shades, her neck of snow?
Twines not of them one golden thread,
But for its sake a Paynim bled.'

"Joy to the fair!—my name unknown,
Each deed, and all its praise thine own
Then, oh! unbar this churlish gate,
The night dew falls, the hour is late.
Inured to Syria's glowing breath,
I feel the north breeze chill as death;
Let grateful love quell maiden shame,
And grant him bliss who brings thee fame."

11 JANUARY

Նա ժամանեց Պաղեստինից՝
Իր մարտական փառքով անբիծ:
Նա մարտերից հոգնաշառաչ
Իր ուսերին բերեց մի խաչ:
Որքա՛ն հեռքեր ունի, որքա՛ն,
Նրա վահանը հաղթական:
Երբ իջնում է մութը երկրին՝
Նա երգում է սիրեցյալին:

«Քո ասպետը, իմ սիրեցյալ
Օտար երկրից եկավ դարձյալ:
Ես չեմ բերել ավար ու փառք,
Իմ նժույգն է զանձա միակ:
Իմ նիզակն է, թուրն իմ փայլուն,
Որով խոցել եմ թշնամուն,
Թող մարտիկը վարձատրվի
Քո ժպիտով՝ այնքա՛ն բարի:

Իմ սիրեցյալ, քո անունով
Անցա մարտի ճամփաներով:
Լոկ դու ես, որ արքունիքում
Պիտի լինես սերն իմ հոգու:
Մունետիկը կազդարարի.
«Տիրուհին է նա սրտերի,
Հանուն նրա՝ գինախաղում
Նետն էր անշեղ առաջ սուրում:

Նրանով էլ ոգեշնչված,
Սուրը խոցեց՝ այսքան կանանց
Զար ամունունւ՝ սուլթանին այն.
Ալլա՛հն էլ չի փրկի նրան:
Մագափունջն է ծփում ոսկյա,
Իսկ մագերին հաշիվ չկա:
Այդքան թվով կռապաշտներ
Ընկան մահով անպատվաբեր»:

Իմ սիրեցյալ, ողջ փառքը քե՛զ,
Փառք ու պատիվ չեմ ուզում ես:
Բա՛ց քո դուռը՝ ներս գամ, անգի՛ն,
Մթնշաղն է պատել այգին,
Ես Սիրիայի շոգից եկել,
Ցուրտ քամուն եմ արդ հանդիպել:
Բա՛ց սենյակիդ դուռն իմ առջեւ.
Քեզ բերել եմ սիրո պարգեւ

12

JANUARY

Inana

My heart is broken,
My soul aches.
Why do I wonder
What is coming next?

Instead of feeling the wind,
Instead of seeing the sun,
Instead of singing the melody
Of my own heart...

Leaves are trembling
Upon temptation of their lives,
Birds are jumping through them
Not thinking much
Of existence, of souls,
Of dark, cold holes
In creatures that once were singing,
Now they call themselves men and women.

I hope someday I will too,
Have meaningless thoughts
And filled heart,
And will just feel the wind,
And the warmth of the sun.

Free like a bird,
Wild as the wind,
I will fly through worlds
As a rootless tree.

14
JANUARY

11 MONDAY

12 TUESDAY

13 WEDNESDAY

14 THURSDAY

15 FRIDAY

16 SATURDAY

17 SUNDAY

TATIANA KULIKOVA (KALMYKIA, RUSSIA)

I'm not ashamed…

The sun has burned its circle out,
Leaving the stars to parade in the sky
And you came by, fooling all no doubt.
My beloved, my dear, you came by.

I will press myself against your chest
In spite of the watching crowd,
Although my conscience says it's not for the best.
"I'm not ashamed," I whisper aloud.

I'm not ashamed. I'll steal just one night
For the lonely longing I've known.
I will hug you. I will hold you tight.
I'll enchant you with my love alone.

"Mine. Only mine!" I intone like a spell
Grateful for my fate bittersweet.
For a happy moment I'm riding the carousel –
"I'm not ashamed," I repeat.

Not ashamed. But lonely, and in love.
I'm just clinging on to some hope.
I've snatched a scrap from the feast above –
I'm human and it's how I cope.

Not ashamed. But my heart is weeping,
Poisoning our minutes of bliss.
All through the night there's bitterness seeping
Into every honeyed kiss.

I will never forget this time with you.
From your touch, my body still moans,
I'm not ashamed. But I want to howl too.
And I will cry on my bed quite alone.

20
JANUARY

Everyone chooses for himself

Everyone chooses for himself
A religion, a woman, a way.
Which devil or prophet today –
Everyone chooses for himself.

Everyone chooses by himself
His words for love and for prayer,
His sword for a duel, the battle he dares.
Everyone chooses by himself.

Everyone chooses by himself.
Shields and armour. His staff and his patches.
And the final reckoning that matches.
Everybody chooses by himself.

Everyone chooses for himself.
And I choose – the best I can.
I've no claim on any man.
Everyone chooses for himself.

*Recommended
by Nadin W. Weklich*

22
JANUARY

Lo que yo quiero

Quiero ser las dos niñas de tus ojos,
las metálicas cuerdas de tu voz,
el rubor de tu sien cuando meditas
y el origen tenaz de tu rubor.

Quiero ser esas manos invisibles
que manejan por sí la Creación,
y formar con tus sueños y los míos
otro mundo mejor para los dos.

Eres tú, providencia de mi vida,
mi sostén, mi refugio, mi caudal:
cual si fueras mi madre yo te amo...
¡y todavía más!

I want to be

I want to be those two girls of your eyes,
That string of your voice when you speak,
I want to be that rose blush on your cheeks,
The one that brings blush to your skin.

I want to be those invisible hands
That make all the world move around,
And shape with those hands and dreams,
yours and mine,
The world that is perfect for us.

I know you're the one: the treasure of mine,
My support, my refuge, my fate.
As a boy seeks his mum, so I love you...
And many times, many times more!

24

JANUARY

18 MONDAY

19 TUESDAY

20 WEDNESDAY

21 THURSDAY

22 FRIDAY

23 SATURDAY					24 SUNDAY

The Twa Corbies (Scottish Song)

As I was walking all alane,
I heard twa corbies making a mane;
The tane unto the t'other say,
'Where sall we gang and dine to-day?'

'In behint yon auld fail dyke,
I wot there lies a new slain knight;
And naebody kens that he lies there,
But his hawk, his hound, and lady fair.

'His hound is to the hunting gane,
His hawk to fetch the wild-fowl hame,
His lady's taen another mate,
So we may mak our dinner sweet.

'Ye'll sit on his white hause-bane,
And I'll pike out his bonny blue een;
Wi ae lock o his gowden hair
We'll theek our nest when it grows bare.

'Mony a one for him makes mane,
But nane sall ken where he is gane;
Oer his white banes, when they are bare,
The wind sall blaw for evermair.'

25
JANUARY

Volkslied (GERMAN)

Ich schweifte umher so ganz allein
Da hört ich zwei Raben schaurig schrein,
Der eine wohl zu dem andern sprach:
Wo finden wir Atzung diesen Tag?

Ich weiß, dort hinter dem faulen Bruch
Liegt ein Ritter erschlagen, frisch genug,
Keine Seele hat ihn dort liegen sehn,
Nur sein Falke sein Hund und sein Liebchen
schön.

Sein Hund der ist nun jagen gangen,
Es will der Falk die Waldvögel fangen,
Das Liebchen hat einen andern erkohren,
Bleibt uns die Mahlzeit doch unverlohren.

Du magst sitzen ihm auf der weißen Brust,
Die süßen blauen Augen pick ich mit Lust,
Eine Locke von seinem goldnen Haar
Flicht das Nest uns aus wenns zerrissen war.

Wohl mancher spricht um ihn traurendes Wort,
Wo er lieget soll keiner wissen den Ort,
Ueber die Knochen wenn nackt und bleich sie sind
Soll ewig hinfahren der kalte Wind.

Translation by Carl August Heinrich Zwicker, 1818

26

JANUARY

Song

Drowsily an aged pine
rustles in her sleep.
Leaning on her coarse-grained trunk
Here I stand and speak.
«little pine-tree, just my age,
Give me of your strength!
Not the usual nine months,
forty years I carried,
forty years I had been bearing,
forty years I had been begging,
begged my heart out, got by pleading,
brought to term
my soul.

Дремлет старая сосна...
Дремлет старая сосна
И шумит со сна.
Я, к шершавому стволу
Прислонясь, стою.
— Сосенка-ровесница,
Передай мне силу!
Я не девять месяцев, —
Сорок лет носила,
Сорок лет вынашивала,
Сорок лет выпрашивала,
Вымолила, выпросила,
Выносила
Душу.

January 28-29, 1926

Translated by
Diana Lewis Burgin

31

JANUARY

25 MONDAY

26 TUESDAY

27 WEDNESDAY

28 THURSDAY

29 FRIDAY

30 SATURDAY

31 SUNDAY

PATRIOTISM INNOMINATUS
(The Lay of the Last Minstrel, Canto VI)

Breathes there the man with soul so dead,
Who never to himself hath said,
'This is my own, my native land!'
Whose heart hath ne'er within him burn'd
As home his footsteps he hath turn'd
From wandering on a foreign strand?
If such there breathe, go, mark him well;
For him no Minstrel raptures swell;
High though his titles, proud his name,
Boundless his wealth as wish can claim;
Despite those titles, power, and pelf,
The wretch, concentred all in self,
Living, shall forfeit fair renown,
And, doubly dying, shall go down
To the vile dust from whence he sprung,
Unwept, unhonour'd, and unsung.

01
FEBRUARY

Pieśń ostatniego minstrela, Pieśń VI
(POLISH)

Jest-że gdzie człowiek, sąż gdzie samoluby,
Co nigdy w sercu, nigdy w myślach swoich,
Nie rzekli z czuciem miłości i chluby:
„To jest ojczyzna, to kraj ojców moich!"
Którychby łzami nie zaszły powieki,
Gdy wspomną o nim w pielgrzymce dalekiéj?
Którychby serce nie, wrzało płomieniem,
Gdy go znów własném obaczą spojrzeniem? —
O! gdy na świecie jest gdzie taki który:
Patrzcie nań, jakby na potwór natury!
I niechby błyszczał choć w mitrze książęcéj,
Niechby miał w skrzyniach tysiące tysięcy:
Mimo tych blasków, tytułów, i złota.
Dział jego będzie: wzgarda za żywota,
I śmierć podwójna — gdy z ciałem pospołu,
I pamięć jego zarzucą do dołu,
Bez czci, bez żalu, bez pieśni nagrobnych,
Na przykład kaźni do niego podobnych!

Translation by
Antoni Edward Odyniec, 1874

04

FEBRUARY

To the Queen of the Ball.

In the chandeliers' soft twilight,
At the far end of the great hall,
Someone raises a toast in delight
To the lovely queen of the ball.

Oh, if only I could tell you truly
How enchanting these nights really are,
If you let yourself merge with each melody,
And stay 'til the morning star.

And tonight's not just for dancing and singing.
It's a celebration – yes, it's your birthday!
And the hall is joyfully ringing
Because you're decked like a gorgeous bouquet!

Happy Birthday, Queen of the Ball!
May the stars give their light to you,
So you may glitter over us all
And shine your whole life through.

07

FEBRUARY

01 MONDAY

02 TUESDAY

03 WEDNESDAY

04 THURSDAY

05 FRIDAY

06 SATURDAY

07 SUNDAY

THE LADY OF THE LAKE Canto IV: I, II

The rose is fairest when 't is budding new,
And hope is brightest when it dawns from fears;
The rose is sweetest washed with morning dew
And love is loveliest when embalmed in tears.
O wilding rose, whom fancy thus endears,
I bid your blossoms in my bonnet wave,
Emblem of hope and love through future years!'
Thus spoke young Norman, heir of Armandave,
What time the sun arose on Vennachar's broad wave.

Such fond conceit, half said, half sung,
Love prompted the bridegroom's tongue.
All while he stripped the wild-rose spray,
His axe and bow beside him lay,
For on a pass 'twixt lake and wood
A wakeful sentinel he stood.

La Donna del Lago IV,
(ITALIAN) **Unknown translator, 1826**

"Vaga e la rosa, quando all'aura olezza
Colle giovani foglie! E piu soave
E la speranza, se di tema e figlia!
Rosa gentil che la rugiada abbella,
Cui vezzi accrebbe fantasia vivace,
Tu m'adorna la fronte, a me di speme
Pegno gentil nell'avvenire incerto!"
D'Armandavo cosi parlo l'erede,
Il giovine Normanno, e il sol spingea
Su Vennaccaro intanto I primi raggi.

Speranza fu, che mormoro gli accenti
Al labbro del Guerrier, mentre dal suolo
Cogliea rosa selvaggia; a lui non lunge,
Tra le stipe giacean l'arco e la scure:
Ch'egli in difficil calle a guardia stasse
Tra lago e bosco…

ELENA KORNEEVA (RUSSIA)

***

Я тебя по карте звёздной для любви нашёл.
Знаю я – ещё не поздно, только снег пошёл,
И следы твои сегодня все запорошил.
Знай, что скоро будет завтра для моей души.
Я тебя найду внезапно, встречу для любви,
И в глазах зелёных нежных утону твоих,
Чтобы снова стать счастливым, но уже навек,
Самый ласковый и верный чудо-человек.

***

On the map of constellations I found you for love.
It's not late – with expectation flakes fall from above.
All your steps in contemplations covered with the snow.
Soon it will become tomorrow for my museful soul.
Then I will forget the sorrow, and for love we'll meet.
In your eyes I will surrender, drown in verdant seas,
To become again delighted, but forever more.
You're affectionate and tender, girl that I adore.

<table>
<tr><td>**14**
FEBRUARY</td></tr>
</table>

08 MONDAY

09 TUESDAY

10 WEDNESDAY

11 THURSDAY

12 FRIDAY

13 SATURDAY

14 SUNDAY

ARMENIAN WOE

Armenian sorrow is a bottomless sea,
A sea of darkness and woe.
And in the depths of my agony,
My soul's drowning far below.

Sometimes, full of rage, it bursts from the sea
And shoots up into the sky.
Then tired of struggle and battle-weary
It plunges to the depths, there to lie.

But I can never plumb the sea bed below
Nor reach up to the sky's top
My soul's wracked in the Armenian sea of woe
And the anguish will never stop.

ՀԱՅՈՑ ՎԻՇՏԸ

Հայոց վիշտը՝ անհուն մի ծով,
Խավար մի ծով ահագին,
Էն սև ծովում տառապելով
Լող է տալիս իմ հոգին:

Մերթ զայրացկոտ ծառս է լինում
Մինչև երկինք կապուտակ
Ու մերթ հոգնած սուզվում, իջնում
Դեպի խորքերն անհատակ:

Ոչ հատակն է գտնում անվերջ
Ու ոչ հասնում երկնքին...
Հայոց վշտի մեծ ծովի մեջ
Տառապում է իմ հոգին:

20

FEBRUARY

This candid poetry collection is clearly the literary outpouring of a planetary citizen. A woman equally at home on the Steppes of Central Asia as much as the Capital cities of Europe. To my mind, a far from trivial verity once we recognise the innate femininity of her versification. Similarly to Sappho (5th Century BC), Nukenova allows everyone access into a woman's world, wherein seductive complexities of thought becomes manifest through wit and rhetoric. Admittedly, her images are often sharp-carefully elaborated for their own jovial sake.

ISBN: 978-1-910886-12-0
RRP: £14.95

21
FEBRUARY

15 MONDAY

16 TUESDAY

17 WEDNESDAY

18 THURSDAY

19 FRIDAY

20 SATURDAY

21 SUNDAY

SAINT CLOUD

Soft spread the southern summer night
Her veil of darksome blue;
Ten thousand stars combined to light
The terrace of Saint Cloud.

The evening breezes gently sigh'd,
Like breath of lover true,
Bewailing the deserted pride
And wreck of sweet Saint Cloud.

The drum's deep roll was heard afar,
The bugle wildly blew
Good-night to Hulan and Hussar
That garrison Saint Cloud.

The startled Naiads from the shade
With broken urns withdrew
And silenced was that proud cascade,
The glory of Saint Cloud.

We sate upon its steps of stone,
Nor could its silence rue
When waked, to music of our own,
The echoes of Saint Cloud.

Slow Seine might hear each lovely note
Fall light as summer dew
While through the moonless air they float
Prolong'd from fair Saint Cloud.

And sure a melody more sweet
His waters never knew,
Though music's self was wont to meet
With Princes at Saint Cloud.

Nor then, with more delighted ear,
The circle round her drew,
Than ours, when gather'd round to hear
Our songstress at Saint Cloud.

Few happy hours poor mortals pass
Then give those hours their due,
And rank among the foremost class
Our evenings at Saint Cloud.

23

FEBRUARY

圣克卢 (CHINESE)

南方夏天的夜拉开
宽阔的深蓝幕，
一万颗星照亮露台
在我的圣克卢。

像恋人的叹息一样
轻柔夜风吹拂，
它想念不再像以往
倒塌的圣克卢。

远方有军号的声音，
有人开始打鼓，
"别送"镇守的骠骑兵
告诉了圣克卢。

美丽那伊阿得斯们
雕像布置马路,
瀑布提示昔日原本
威严的圣克卢。

我们坐着在阶梯上
聆听音乐倾诉，
尚且肃静聆听人弹
在我的圣克卢。

塞纳也听每个曲调
滴落如露水珠，
音符飘在夜晚的霄，
回响在圣克卢。

河岸边从来没人唱
那么美的旋律，
声音胜过王子欣赏
的歌在圣克卢。

虽然过去的人珍惜
无数的各种曲，
我们仍特别的欢喜
悦耳的圣克卢。

多年辛苦，少日快乐，
然后告别归土。
在我的少日中有了
夜晚在圣克卢。

26

FEBRUARY

MIKHAIL LERMONTOV (RUSSIA)

The Prophet

Since the everlasting judge indeed
Gave me a prophet's keen insight,
In people's eyes, I now must read
Bitter pages of vice and spite.

I proclaim to them the purity
That is found in truth and love,
But the stones my neighbours throw at me
Still rain down from above.

I coat my head in ash and grime –
Run a beggar from the city.
And now I live in a desert clime
On what God gives in his pity.

My pact with the eternal one holds true –
The beasts obey me here.
And the stars, they listen to me too –
Their rays dance joyful and clear.

But when through a noisy town again,
I slide hastily on my way,
The elders smile on with disdain
And to their children say:

"Let him be an example to you – see!
Too proud to live among us,
The fool kept telling us endlessly
That God speaks with his tongue.

So look at him, children, look how grim –
How pale and thin and sore!
How threadbare is this wretch, and poor –
How everyone despises him."

28

FEBRUARY

22 MONDAY

23 TUESDAY

24 WEDNESDAY

25 THURSDAY

26 FRIDAY

27 SATURDAY

28 SUNDAY

TATIANA VASILIEVA (RUSSIA / KAZAKHSTAN)

I think that…

If you stir the water
For a long time in one direction,
You can whisper spells into it.
Water will endure everything.

Like a wave hitting the coast,
It will deliver my words to the world.
And the world will resound, unable to
Resist its constituent essence.

Like a swift wings through the sky,
The word rushes out from the speaker's chest
And, entangled in the play of waters
As in a hunter's trap, seeks to

Leave the world that gave birth to it.
Like white sea foam, the word beats against
The shores of meaning, not letting the world
Remain the same…

03
MARCH

The Silence

Early morning.
My gut denies the existence of the alarm clock.
You who invented it be so kind as to take your idea back.
My revolt was beyond measures of propriety.

At random, my head is at the edge of the bed,
and my eyes start following the movements of Silence;
my sleepy legs lash over three pile blocks.

From the oven to the bar table and back.
The Silence is making coffee.
Before pouring it into cups, it tests me for vigor.

The moment it leaves the tiles and steps on the shag carpet,
I pretend to be asleep. The test disappoints and
melts me at the same time.

Disappointment from the thought
that I will have to have breakfast alone,
and the melt from the sight of my beloved asleep.

With a sad smile, the Silence returned
to have a coffee alone. Easily climbing a bar chair
it starts the day full of artistic activity.

Lazy curls scrambled together, L-size T-shirt,
distance spectacles, a colored Ikea cup
are the advisors to the Silence.

They all together respond to the messages
hanging in the spaces of neon networks.
It's time for me to get up and disturb the Silence
with my "morning kindness."

Translated by
Tatiana Vasilieva
(Russia – Kazakhstan)

To Draw a Novel. To Write a Picture.

The painter's hands show us the world.
Constant doubts in himself are reflected in fine
lines.
Slight shivering of past quarrels.

By pressing a little harder on the watercolour paper,
she wanted to trace her confidence.
The softest tones depicted her dreams.

Those airy clouds… she wanted to be
as light when falling asleep.
Early dawns in soft frames,

A slow waltz of brushes and fingers
at the whitest dance floor.
Too strict on your talent but you'll reconcile,
won't you?

The writer's words deliver the prays.
About the portraits left in an empty apartment;
the neck bends in the letters; the smells are like
cooking recipes.

The collected works uncover themselves
chapter after another; grating phrases,
delicate hints.
You'll read this, won't you?
And no one will understand us.

They won't recognize themselves in the colours;
they won't hear their own voice in the paragraphs.
Thoughts roughed by pillow spill out into the rivers
of waiting.

We are lost in ports in the search for the ocean
that contains the answers. Kilometers chew themselves as tapes in a tape recorder.

The time has sailed away aboard the first ferry.
It's too early to smile, and to part forever each time.
It is always calm before the storm.

Translated by
Tatiana Vasilieva (Russia – Kazakhstan)

07

MARCH

01 MONDAY

02 TUESDAY

03 WEDNESDAY

04 THURSDAY

05 FRIDAY

06 SATURDAY

07 SUNDAY

SARIA MAMMADOVA (AZERBAIJAN)

Phrases and Quotes of Saria Mammadova.

• Under the influence of cultural masterpieces, books, education and proper upbringing some people are able to form and enrich their interior life. That inner world can become so deep and pure that ignorance, impersonality and incompetence of others is incapable of harming it.

• A person should constantly continue following his/her self-development path in order to improve himself/herself at every stage of his/her life's journey.

• Reading is forming particular spiritual and cultural values and ideals in the morality of human being. This type of morality can never be banalized by the negative and simply ignorant information provided by some media and TV channels.

08

MARCH

From the poem "A brief romance"

His dear girl's lovely figure,
Her ardent eyes shining bright,
Her youth full of flame and vigour
And love's sorcery gave him boundless delight.
The lure of ripe female flesh
And the country life's pleasantness,
And the simple charm of the ordinary,
Called him to her irresistibly,
Anticipating that sweet time
When in silent seclusion she
Is alone with him entirely,
Shy, half naked, sublime,
And languid, drunk so sweetly,
She trusts to him completely.

13
MARCH

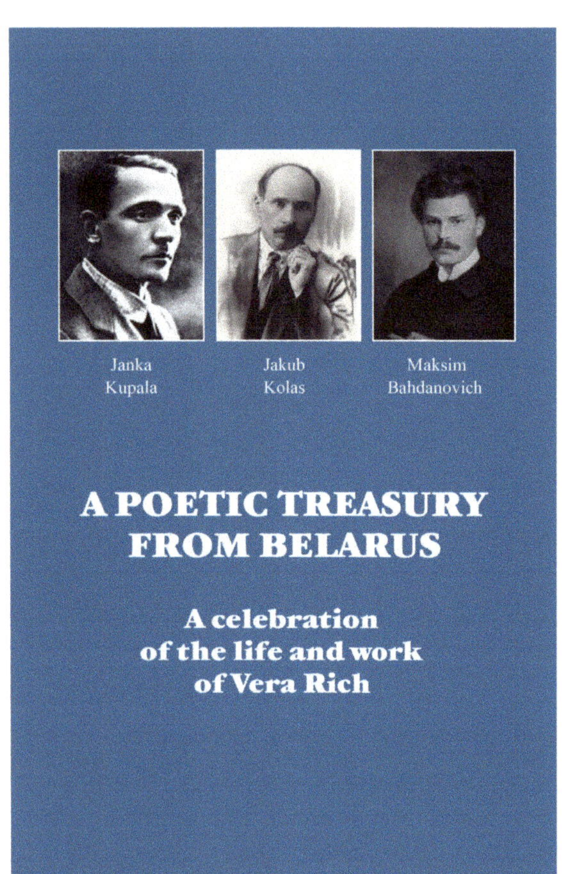

In this adventurous poetic treasury, three remarkable word-smiths from Belarus are further introduced to specialists and general anglophone readers alike. A feat only realisable, possibly, through the outstanding vision and almost legendry skills of translator, journalist, songsmith and cultural historian, Vera Rich. Indeed, her insightful, pioneering, work on the potent and stirring verses of Janka Kupala - the bard and prophet of Belarusian letters, is herein accompanied by subtle interpretations of Jakub Kolas as the wry observer of Belarusian customs, along with Maksim Bahdanovich as its experimental, sophisticated and lyrical literary moderniser. Each fearless poet, in turn, constructing the very foundations upon which contemporary Belarusian literature is built. And as such, this proud collection of captivating poetry from a uniquely gifted nation truly celebrates the achievements of an astonishing lady.

ISBN: 978-1-913356-04-0
RRP: £14.95

14
MARCH

08 MONDAY

09 TUESDAY

10 WEDNESDAY

11 THURSDAY

12 FRIDAY

13 SATURDAY   14 SUNDAY

Tell me Homeland, what have you done for us?

Place where I was born saying "Ingak" – you are sacred and my native land!
I pressed your soil to my eye and thanked God infinitely.
I endured such hardship and suffering until I came back to you.
But tell me Homeland, what have you done for me?

You took everything from my grandfather, unjustly shot, saying that you are rich.
You arrested my father and sent him to the Far East for years,
defaming him as a supporter of Trotsky,
And you oppressed my mother for her close relationship with Al-Khorazmiy,
considering her dangerous.
Tell me Motherland, if the ancestors asked you on the day of judgment,
what would you say to them?

My generation comes from Oguz-khan, Al-Khorazmiy, Mahdumkuli-Fraghi.
I received religious and secular knowledge from religious and secular scholars to perfection.
I received my Sufi knowledge from Hamadani, Kubro, Naqshband and Dzhushan.
For the sake of the saints, tell me Homeland truthfully, what have you done for me?

I worked exhausted, from dawn to dark, never knowing rest,
I sprayed Demeton and DDT with my bare hands, and I was poisoned for a long time,
My arm was broken in the fields, and I lay unconscious in the hospital for many days,
Look at me Motherland, and tell me, in the bleakest days what have you done for me?

To preserve the soil of my homeland, I studied for years and became a scientist.
To increase productivity for my people, I overcame many difficulties to become a chemist.
For my homeland, I became a writer and singer, and wrote and sang without stopping.
Tell me Motherland with faith, what have you done for your patriotic son?

I was not interested in politics and power; my role was work, creativity and science.
I did not pursue a career; I aimed at leadership to serve the people.
I did not think about accumulating wealth. My lifestyle and food were simple.
Homeland, why did you ignore the poor and flatter the rich and officials?

15

MARCH

In the interests of my people, I fought against corruption and wrote the book "Commissioner" (Vakil),
Because of this, I was deprived of employment and expelled from Khorezm too,
Because of the purity of the biosphere of his homeland, I became an enemy to Karimov's regime.
Why then did you not take his head, and not save me, his patriotic son?

I went to the Hajj, hugged the Kaaba and prayed for my homeland, wishing him good luck.
I shed tears at the grave of the Messenger of Allah and prayed for my people for a long time,
When Karimov was chasing the pilgrims, I remained unemployed and cried bitterly.
Tell me, Motherland, what have you done to protect me, Haji?

When the communists said build a luxury house for the party, I built a mosque.
I landscaped cemeteries, and made tombs for the saints.
For my people, I gave land, built roads, dug wells and brought water.
What did you do, homeland, when atheists humiliated me for this?

I accepted my destiny from God and worked day and night without limit,
I was grateful for each day, read the Quran and prayed with all my heart,
I experienced difficulties, held "Bis-Sabr" firmly and was patient,
Tell me Homeland, what have you done to give hope for a better day?

When I wanted to go my Homeland, the Foreign Ministry said "give thanks" to us, as it should.
When I repeatedly addressed the President, he said give them more.
When I said that giving a bribe is a crime, they said: then die of homesickness.
Tell me Homeland, is this the reform that your supporters proclaim?

When I wrote my Selected Works in more than 20 volumes, you called me a great scientist.
When I wrote dozens of works in prose and poetry, you called me a great writer.
In your press you praised me, saying: Praise you "The Pride of Khorezm!"
Tell me Homeland, what did you do when your corruption humiliated me?

If I were a poet, I would write as In a proverb: "A friend speaks bitterly."
The tongues of your poets are tied, and sit as if they have chewed wax.
Your praisers sing praises, scattering saliva from their mouths.
Tell me Homeland honestly, how much did you give them cash in green (dollar)?

When I was over 70, you destroyed my family and broke our lives for bribes.
You spread the scandalous "Attack and bite!" and you made children orphans.
Using the mafia and threatening "we'll kill you!" you ignored my appeals,
UK-Homeland tell me, is this your European democratic justice?

Tell me, it's my fault that I am the descendants of Adam and Oguzkhan.
Or it's my fault that, I come from generations of Al-Khorazmiy and Firagi.
Or is it my fault that I am faithful to the scholars and the Sufi,
Hey Motherlands, tell me what is my fault, why you are humiliating me so much?

*

When Khorazmiy was born, he clearly heard the sound of Adhan, the name and greatness of God,
At the age of 3, he recited the Quran many times with his teacher,
At the age of 5, he knew by heart half the God's words - the Quran,
So Motherland, why didn't you support him, and say "Mashallah!"?

At the age of 4 years, he taught people about Islam and made them literate,
He memorized all chemistry for his exams, and stunned the examiners.
At the age of 30, he received the title of laureate of the Academy of Sciences Prize and surprised scientists.
Tell me Homeland, what have you done for your extraordinarily gifted son?

He received a blessing in uvaysi from Karani, Hamadani, Naqshband and Zhushan.
He practiced Sufism and tariqah day and night, and performed a prayers with difficulty.
In tasavwuf, using his knowledge, he founded the tariqa "Naqshbandiya-Khorazmiy",
What have you done as a homeland for such a righteous Sufi?

He was able to conquer Asia, Africa and Europe, and he was fluent in 10 languages.
In 5 languages of the world he wrote treatises and books which became bestsellers,
He composed music to poems, and sang them in many languages
on a musical instrument – the tar.
Tell me Motherland, what have you done for the perfection of your son,
the conqueror of half the world?

17

MARCH

As a strong man, he raised a man on one arm and received applause,
In the medical board, he squeezed the doctor's hand, broke it and became a student.
He played Nigel Short in chess, and almost took his champion's title,
Well, Motherland, what have you done to develop your son, an athlete?

Was there such a scientist, who wrote four doctoral dissertations in four different disciplines,
Was there such a scientist, who recognized as "Khorezm's Dokuchaev",
Was anyone other than Zamakhshari named as "Pride of Khorezm",
So, why didn't you value them, Motherland?

He was not afraid when Karimov said: "Arrest or destroy him!"
He was not afraid when the mafia in England gave him a threatening letter "We will kill you!"
He accepted his fate when the doctors said: "the operation on his heart is complicated",
Tell me Motherland, did you support your such brave son?

Most of the mahalla and mosques that he built, remain in his name.
He wrote many phrases in different languages, which became tips and slogans.
Karimov stole some of these words, and put his name on them.
If you are the Motherland, why didn't you let such a son and patriot into his home?

Isn't this the hero who went against the politicians for you?
Is this not the scientist who made widely recognized discoveries and inventions?,
Didn't his "Vakil" (Commissioner) become the "Gulag", and he "Solzhenitsyn"?
If you are a true Motherland, where is your "Solzhenitsyn"?

He argued that film should not use the Andijan and the Chinese method, but the Uzbekistan method,
going against Karimov.
He said agricultural technology should be based on soil, fertilization, climate and science.
He also said that ecology should absolutely outweigh plans, productivity, and even the economy,
Oh, illiterate and ignorant Motherland, why didn't you defend the scientist who told the truth?

18
MARCH

Who, as a deputy , argued with the authorities who introduced toxic chemicals to a remote place.
Who, as a scientist, first showed the inconsistency of the leader-Lenin's theory,
Who, as a Sufi, refused to enjoy worldly pleasures and so was humiliated,
Tell me Homeland, what have you done for your universal son?

Have you supported Genghis, who said: "Turks unite!"?
Did you support Khorazmiy, who said: "Unite the Khorezm's people!"?
Did you support your Sufi who said: "Sufism is not a religion, but science loves God"?
Tell me, if you are a true homeland, what have you done for them?

Didn't you know that, he was a guest worker abroad for you?
Didn't you see that when he was starving in a foreign country he had to live on garbage?
Didn't you hear that he gave all his money to you and ate herbs himself?
Shameless Motherland, when you heard all this, did your conscience torment you?

The mothers of your children were arrested saying: "Give bribes or get 5 years in prison",
No one heard the complaints of the 10-14 year old disabled children left alone and cared for,
The Homeland did not hear the suffering of these orphans, crying at the doors of so many people,
Oh, bribetaker Motherland, how can this be the fault of children – is this your motherhood?

You forced Khorezmiy leave the country, then called him a traitor.
You left his relatives and children unemployed, terrorized and imprisoned them.
You destroyed his grave, you spread fear to people, and you ignored his complaints.
Oh, Motherland, you slanderer who will live in history as a "destroyer of the grave" – is this your motherhood?

Turkmenbashi said: "Such a scientist is alone in Uzbekistan, and he is also Turkmen".
Your Yurtbashi said: "If there is a distortion in the press, then arrest the journalist;
if this is correct, then rewrite the Khorazmiy document as not Uzbek."
If you are not a nationalist, why didn't you say that the Uzbek and Turkmen
are equal as citizens?

19
MARCH

When you left him hungry with a 30 dollar salary, your scientist-professor was lost in the market.
The Kazakhs also ridiculed your scientist and said: "For 100 dollars, look after our sheep."
Turkmenistan also told him: "You didn't come when you were invited, now suffer."
Oh, the shameless Motherland, at least once did you remember your scientist whom you humiliated?

The badawi Arabs did not appreciate the Prophet – and landed in trouble,
Rulers of seven countries argued over the body of Uvais Karani - and found benefits.
If the Homelands do not appreciate Khorazmiy, God will punish them without doubt.
Oh Motherland, will not it be as the proverb says: "What you don't value, the same you will need?"

The world knew that he himself did not eat, and generously sacrificed everything that he had to the needy and the sick,
Khorezm, Turkmenistan, Evril Turon in Tashkent received the benefits of his generosity,
Six year-old Farogat, who suffered from leukaemia, also said: "Thank you, father., for your generosity!",
Homeland, did you ever show kindness to the magnanimous Khatamtai in his difficult days?

Dr. Smith, who was planning to teach him, became a Muslim and took lessons from him,
Atheist Daniel became a Muslim and named his son 'Akhmad' in his honour.
Many people who have gone astray have come to the right path thanks to the teachings of Khorazmiy.
Oh, stupid and ungrateful Motherland, when will you also apologize and step on the right path?

The poet Salih wrote: "He wrote his books well on the basis of documents, unfortunately they were not published."
Famous scientist Polvon said: "His works became famous, but he remained humble."
The writer Annakuli said: "He worked hard all his life, yet his entire wealth was knowledge and faith."
Tell me Motherland freak, aren't these fair assessments of your son that you didn't give?

He received a lot of knowledge from Abdullah kari, Sergey Ryzhov, Jura Sattarov.
He received the fatwa: "Bon voyage in literature!" from Genghis, Isa, Annakuli and Khaldar,
He was educated in leadership and struggle by Iskandar Dosov, Sapo-fighter and Tulanboy.
Well, Motherland, did you at least respect his teachers?

20
MARCH

When he said: "One must accept – God's destiny," his disciples agreed, God's destiny,
When he said: "One must be grateful – for each day", believers were at once grateful for each day.
When he said: "One must have patience – for the difficulties of life," his followers had patience with the difficulties of life.
When he said: "You need to have hope - for a good day," you Motherland, did you also have hope for a good day?

God in his book said to his slaves: "There is no God but Me, Muhammad is my Messenger",
The Prophet (saw) told his ummah: "Ayat-ul-Kursi is the leader of the verses of the words of Allah."
Sheikh Khorazmiy told his students: "Al-Fatiha is the leader of the Qur'anic surah; the Qur'an is the leader of the books of Allah,"
Ah, you unscrupulous homeland, why did you say to your citizens: "Bow to the Pharaohs!"?

Khorazmiy's appeal to scientists and people of the world gave the world a real warning,
What he wrote about tasawwuf , he woke the ulama and the Sufis,
With his knowledge, Sheikh Khorazmiy opened a new path to tasawwuf,
Shameless Homeland, why did you envy him instead of admiring?

If you were the true homeland, the Khorezmians would not leave Khorezm.
If you were brave, Beruni wouldn't have stayed in Ghazna.
If you were kind, your children would not leave you.
In fairness tell me Homeland who mowed your raw barley?

Is it your motherhood that made Halima and Gulchehra cry?
Is it your paternity that expelled Bukhari from his homeland?
Is it your justice that persecuted Salihs, driving them from their land?
If you have a conscience, Motherland, have you asked them for forgiveness?

<table>
<tr><td>

21

MARCH

</td><td>

The Khorezmians with their knowledge made Khorezm great in the world.
The Bukharians made Bukhara, located in the desert, honourable in Islam.
Yassavians wrote wisdom that made Turkestan famous.
For God's sake, tell me Homeland, what have you done for them?

</td></tr>
</table>

15 MONDAY

16 TUESDAY

17 WEDNESDAY

18 THURSDAY

19 FRIDAY

20 SATURDAY   21 SUNDAY

A dance of swans

Somewhere beyond the fields of green barley,
In a quiet place, by a mirror lake,
Two snow-white birds are dancing gracefully,
Displaying their courtship for the daybreak.

Splashing the still waters far and wide,
Beating his wings and bowing his head,
The groom confronts his desired bride,
Spraying the shining pearls that he's shed.

The female swan, girlish and shy,
Lowers her head so gracefully too,
Then, pristine in her white lace, sighs
And says to her sweetheart softly, "I do".

Finally, long, slender necks entwining,
Fluffing their feathers up in a spray,
Swan and swan dance in the morning
Pledging eternal love in their way.

22
MARCH

Motherhood.

I've left my working schedule and tedious meetings behind,
But I'm suffering new ailments, and anxiety grips my mind.
Yet inside me a flower grows; it's taking root within.
It gives me strength, and soon I know, my new life will begin.

This bright flower is Motherhood! It is life's call eternal.
It brings with it a true welcome and a complete renewal.
And this fragile living thing rests on your little shoulders
But it makes sure you're never beaten and your fire always smoulders.

I want to live and breathe again; and new hope fills my soul.
I embrace the world with all my heart to comfort and console.
And with a soft and friendly smile the moon will send its beams
And through the years it will remind me of my youthful dreams.

24
MARCH

NATALIE BISSO (GERMANY)

A house in the mountains.

Well, here I am on my own – just me.
I'll light a fire and collapse in a seat.
My insights can curl up the chimney;
My past thoughts can go in the heat.

I'll take it now at the slowest of paces;
There's no need to hurry any more.
By refining to perfect, filigree phrases,
I will surely come to the core.

When Spring is in a fluster.

What does the year have to say
If spring takes your every day?
Spring in your soul, spring in your eyes,
Spring mirrored in every sunrise.

Blessed be the day and blessed the hour
When love took you wholly in its power.
Let it fill your heart with its warm rays,
Intoxicate you with each new day.

Love is such a miracle for all.
It makes the very world seem small!
And the world is changed, the wind veers,
And the heart fills with new hope's cheer.

In every moment, every trace,
Is drawn a sweet and gentle face.
Let your life be filled with laughter
And with love forever after!

25
MARCH

22 MONDAY

23 TUESDAY

24 WEDNESDAY

25 THURSDAY

26 FRIDAY

27 SATURDAY   28 SUNDAY

My Angel's voice

It's late at night.
My quaint dream
Unfolds itself in an endless scream.

I want to curse,
But not to bless
The cloudy stream of consciousness.

No use! No sight!
And more... No hope!
But in the dark I've got to cope.

My heart is calling,
I'm aflame!
Someone is whispering my name.

A sparkling breath
To balm my soul!
Bring back the light that darkness stole!

My Angel's voice!
This hallow flow
Will give me rest and let things go.

30
MARCH

The simple answer

Forgive my sins, forget my past.
This sacred moment will not last.
Repeat my name, reclaim my soul.
Sometimes we start to lose control.

I have to learn, I have to trust.
We are within a stone's cast.
Yet far away my thoughts exist.
You clasp the bracelet round my wrist.

I'm trapped within a golden cage.
My heart darkens in its rage.
Why shouldn't I make my adieu?
Your answer's simple – "I love you"

31
MARCH

The Wanderers

When heaven was burning icon lamps
Over woods, meadow and lakes
There was a falling of grains of stars!
Like carnelians, it rained on the land.

Like bright emeralds, jasper and opals
Spilling down from the sky in cold sparks
Over mountains, sheer cliffs immortal
Hidden by the clouds in their wrath.

For being hid from the inescapable fate
In a fleeting free fall they moved
Like the perfidy of The Last Supper they were
Into thorns that only were soft.

Into the ground they crashed turning tares up
Then sprouted so abundantly in dense shoots
In the North and the South so spreadingly
The whole world quickly stopped being rough.

02
APRIL

A Stranger

An unknown girl sits in the square
Silent, but weeping uncontrollably.
Her soul not crushed but stripped bare,
Ripped to pieces horribly.

No she is not dreaming it –
She's a young eagle caught fast,
A sinner hurled into a pit
To be battered with each stone cast.

No, no, she's a soft turtledove
That's smashed into the ground.
I wish to say, "You can start again, love!"
But just listen without a sound.

03
APRIL

A prize-winning poem by Moldovan author, Ludmila Dubcovetcaia, Rhymes about Boys is a vibrant tour de force. Joyful and witty in equal measure, this engaging and fast-paced book is bound to captivate children. Can you find your name in there?

ISBN: 978-1-913356-03-3
RRP: £22.50

04
APRIL

29 MONDAY

30 TUESDAY

31 WEDNESDAY

01 THURSDAY

02 FRIDAY

03 SATURDAY

04 SUNDAY

Nothing is so beautiful as Spring –
   When weeds, in wheels, shoot long and lovely and lush;
   Thrush's eggs look little low heavens, and thrush
Through the echoing timber does so rinse and wring
The ear, it strikes like lightnings to hear him sing;
   The glassy peartree leaves and blooms, they brush
   The descending blue; that blue is all in a rush
With richness; the racing lambs too have fair their fling.

What is all this juice and all this joy?
   A strain of the earth's sweet being in the beginning
In Eden garden. – Have, get, before it cloy,
   Before it cloud, Christ, lord, and sour with sinning,
Innocent mind and Mayday in girl and boy,
   Most, O maid's child, thy choice and worthy the winning.

07

APRIL

TO ARINA

I know a girl in Odessa
Down by the black, black sea.
She's eyes as dark as coffee
And she's waiting there for me.

One day I'll make an odyssey
Down to Odessa's sea.
Like Homer's hero, coming home:
That's just how it will be!

Maybe I will come in spring
When blossom clothes the trees,
And the air is gently humming
With the sound of eager bees.

Odessa then becomes a bride
All dressed in pink and white,
Just waiting for the moment
When Odysseus comes in sight.

Of course I am no champion
No soldier from back then.
I'm just a humble man of words
Armed only with a pen.

But I will come to find that girl
With eyes as dark as tea
And win in love's arena
Down by the black, black sea.

09
APRIL

YULIANA PROTASOVA (UK)

Я сошью тебе платье из гроздей пахучей сирени,
Я украшу ромашками блузу из ласковых роз,
Я вплету тебе в косы райской птицы высокие трели,
Я влюбилась в тебя на всю жизнь абсолютно всерьёз.

Я умою лицо прохладной водой родниковой,
Обогрею лучами далеких небесных светил,
Расплету тебе косы, и ветром сомненья развею.
Я люблю тебя так, как ещё никто не любил.

Нарумянит лицо свежий воздух и яркое солнце,
Искупает потоком воды тебя дождь проливной,
Напою тебя досыта чистейшей водой ключевою,
Буду сказки шептать летней ночью тебе под луной.

Огражу светом молний от бедствий-препятствий, укрою,
Убаюкает в сон сладкозвучная музыка вод,
И мечтать научу: беспредельно и сладко, со мною
Глядя в звездный бескрайний волшебный судьбы небосвод.

I will make you a dress from bunches of fragrant lilacs,
I will decorate your blouse with tender roses,
I will weave plumes from a bird of paradise in your braids,
I fell in love with you forever, absolutely and seriously.

I will wash your face with cool spring water,
I will warm you with rays of heavenly light,
I will untie your braids, and I will scatter your doubts with the wind.
I love you like no one else has loved.

Fresh air and bright sun will blush your face,
I will bath you in the pouring rain,
I will give you to drink pure spring water,
I will whisper fairy-tales on a summer night to you under the moon.

I will protect you with lightning and thunder from obstacles and disasters,
The sweet-sounding music of the waters will lull you to sleep,
And I will teach you how to dream: infinitely and sweetly, with me
Looking at the starry boundless magical sky of fate.

11

APRIL

05 MONDAY

06 TUESDAY

07 WEDNESDAY

08 THURSDAY

09 FRIDAY

10 SATURDAY

11 SUNDAY

LOCHINVAR (Marmion Canto V)

O, young Lochinvar is come out of the west,
Through all the wide Border his steed was the best;
And save his good broadsword, he weapons had none,
He rode all unarm'd, and he rode all alone.
So faithful in love, and so dauntless in war,
There never was knight like the young Lochinvar.

He staid not for brake, and he stopp'd not for stone,
He swam the Eske river where ford there was none;
But ere he alighted at Netherby gate,
The bride had consented, the gallant came late:
For a laggard in love, and a dastard in war,
Was to wed the fair Ellen of brave Lochinvar.

So boldly he entered the Netherby Hall,
Among bride's-men, and kinsmen, and brothers, and all:
Then spoke the bride's father, his hand on his sword,
(For the poor craven bridegroom said never a word,)
"O come ye in peace here, or come ye in war,
Or to dance at our bridal, young Lord Lochinvar?"--
"I long woo'd your daughter, my suit you denied;--
Love swells like the Solway, but ebbs like its tide--
And now am I come, with this lost love of mine,

To lead but one measure, drink one cup of wine.
There are maidens in Scotland more lovely by far,
That would gladly be bride to the young Lochinvar."

The bride kiss'd the goblet; the knight took it up,
He quaff'd off the wine, and he threw down the cup.
She look'd down to blush, and she look'd up to sigh,
With a smile on her lips, and a tear in her eye.
He took her soft hand, ere her mother could bar,--
"Now tread we a measure!" said young Lochinvar.

So stately his form, and so lovely her face,
That never a hall such a galliard did grace;
While her mother did fret, and her father did fume,
And the bridegroom stood dangling his bonnet and plume;
And the bride-maidens whisper'd, " 'Twere better by far
To have match'd our fair cousin with young Lochinvar."

One touch to her hand, and one word in her ear,
When they reach'd the hall-door, and the charger stood near;
So light to the croupe the fair lady he swung,
So light to the saddle before her he sprung!
"She is won! we are gone, over bank, bush, and scaur;
They'll have fleet steeds that follow," quoth young Lochinvar.
There was mounting 'mong Graemes of the Netherby clan;
Fosters, Fenwicks, and Musgraves, they rode and they ran:
There was racing and chasing, on Cannobie Lee,
But the lost bride of Netherby ne'er did they see.
So daring in love, and so dauntless in war,
Have ye e'er heard of gallant like young Lochinvar?

12

APRIL

Lochinvar (FRENCH)

Beau Lochinvar, fleur de chevalerie,
Qui ne rendit hommage à ta valeur ?
Qui n'envia le sort de ton amie ?
Qui n'eût voulu te devoir le bonheur ?

Il a volé sur son coursier rapide,
Des ennemis il a percé les rangs,
Gravi les monts et franchi les torrens ;
Honneur, amour, à l'amant intrépide !

De Netherby le gothique manoir
Frappe sa vue au retour de l'aurore ;
Son cœur bondit ! C'est son Eléonore
Que le guerrier aujourd'hui vient revoir.

Soumise, hélas ! aux volontés d'un père,
Eléonore a formé d'autres nœuds,
Et c'est ce soir qu'un hymen odieux
Doit affliger un amant si sincère.

Mais Lochinvar s'avance avec fierté ;
Lâche rival, l'époux de l'infidèle,
Baissant les yeux, à son père irrité
Laisse le soin de venger sa querelle.

— Dans ce château venez-vous en ami,
Dit le vieillard, ou nous porter la guerre ?
Le preux répond : — Votre fille a trahi
Tous les sermens qu'elle me fit naguère.

Mais en Ecosse il est mainte beauté
Qui pour époux m'accepterait encore ;

Je ne viens point troubler votre gaîté ;
Je viens danser avec Eléonore.

Lui dire adieu voilà tout mon désir ;
Regrette-t-on une amante légère ? —
Elle rougit, elle pousse un soupir ;
Larme d'amour vint mouiller sa paupière.

Sans hésiter Lochinvar prend sa main,
Et puis gaîment il se mêle à la danse.
Chacun tout bas dit : — Gloire au paladin
Qui réunit la grace et la vaillance !

Mais Lochinvar n'a dit qu'un mot tout bas
En regardant la jeune fiancée ;
Éléonore a compris sa pensée :
Il sort, bientôt elle a suivi ses pas.

Ils sont déjà sur le coursier rapide.
Courez, volez, hôtes de ce château :
Ils ont déjà dépassé le coteau !
On ne vit plus cet amant intrépide.

Qui ne rendit hommage à ta valeur,
Beau Lochinvar, fleur de chevalerie ?
Qui n'envia le sort de ton amie ?
Qui n'eût voulu le devoir le bonheur ?

*Translation by Auguste-Jean-
Baptiste Defauconpret, 1820*

13
APRIL

Hanba

Ja plakal som nad sudbou Sláva,
no zmĺkol plač i zmĺkol spev.
A v dlane rúk mi klesla hlava.
Žiaľ nezhynul a búri hnev
a odberá mi pokoj duši,
o rode spev môj predsa čuší.

I milujem ja jednu krásku.
Hľa, nad rodom som neplakal,
a ako k deve cítim lásku,
ju ospevujem, bôľ i žiaľ.
Ó, zmĺkni spev. Ó, zmlčte muky!
Vypadni pero z trasnej ruky!

Shame

I long wept for the glory of Fame,
But then my song and cry were hushed.
My hands covered my face in shame.
Alas, unchecked, my anger flashed
And took my peace, my soul was hurt.
My song about us still is heard.

I sang love songs and deeply sighed,
When with one girl I fell in love.
About my nation, have I cried?
Now I feel pain on its behalf.
O, hush my song! O, hush my pain!
O, hand! Don't you dare write again!

14
APRIL

12 MONDAY

13 TUESDAY

14 WEDNESDAY

15 THURSDAY

16 FRIDAY

17 SATURDAY

18 SUNDAY

WHY SIT'ST THOU BY THAT RUIN'D HALL

'Why sit'st thou by that ruin'd hall,
Thou aged carle so stern and grey?
Dost thou its former pride recall,
Or ponder how it pass'd away?'-

'Know'st thou not me?' the Deep Voice cried;
'So long enjoy'd, so oft misused-
Alternate, in thy fickle pride,
Desired, neglected, and accused!

'Before my breath, like blazing flax,
Man and his marvels pass away!
And changing empires wane and wax,
Are founded, flourish, and decay,

'Redeem mine hours - the space is brief -
While in my glass the sand-grains shiver,
And measureless thy joy or grief,
When Time and thou shalt part for ever!'

21
APRIL

Старче, що ти правиш там? (BULGARIAN)

Хей, старче! Що ти правиш там
край разрушената стена?
Припомняш славата й май,
или как край я сполетя?

"Не знаеш ли аз кой съм? - глас
дълбок и громък зазвуча. -
Тъй често радват ми се, аз
съм често злобно поруган.

Дъхът ми, като лен горящ,
изгаря теб и твоя вик;
империи, царе искрящ
той покосява в кратък миг.

Използвай времето си ти -
защото пясъкът изтича, -
за радост, мъка и мечти,
преди вий да се разделите.

Translation by Irina Petrova

22
APRIL

OLD LETTERS

How I love a lazy rustle
Of old letters, of the past ...
There's a smell of drying blossom,
There's a beauty that won't last.

How I love the weave of writing,
I can hear the dry leaves swish.
Swiftly written lines are hiding
Whispers of a yearning wish.

Their sound is so dear to me,
Their weary blissful charm...
They're the tree of Knowledge blooming
And the evening thoughtful calm.

23
APRIL

19 MONDAY

20 TUESDAY

21 WEDNESDAY

22 THURSDAY

23 FRIDAY

24 SATURDAY   25 SUNDAY

Η ΠΟΛΙΣ

Είπες· «Θα πάγω σ' άλλη γη, θα πάγω σ' άλλη θάλασσα.
Μια πόλις άλλη θα βρεθεί καλύτερη από αυτή.
Κάθε προσπάθεια μου μια καταδίκη είναι γραφτή·
κι είν' η καρδιά μου — σαν νεκρός — θαμμένη.
Ο νους μου ώς πότε μες στον μαρασμόν αυτόν θα μένει.
Όπου το μάτι μου γυρίσω, όπου κι αν δω
ερείπια μαύρα της ζωής μου βλέπω εδώ,
που τόσα χρόνια πέρασα και ρήμαξα και χάλασα.»

Καινούριους τόπους δεν θα βρεις, δεν θά βρεις άλλες θάλασσες.
Η πόλις θα σε ακολουθεί. Στους δρόμους θα γυρνάς
τους ίδιους. Και στες γειτονιές τες ίδιες θα γερνάς·
και μες στα ίδια σπίτια αυτά θ' ασπρίζεις.
Πάντα στην πόλι αυτή θα φθάνεις. Για τα αλλού — μη ελπίζεις —
δεν έχει πλοίο για σε, δεν έχει οδό.
Έτσι που τη ζωή σου ρήμαξες εδώ
στην κόχη τούτη την μικρή, σ' όλην την γη την χάλασες.

1910

29
APRIL

THE TOWN

You said: "I'll find another land,
I'll sail another sea,
And there I'll find a better town
Than this, from which I flee.
Here, nothing I try to do
Will ever find success.
My heart feels as if it's dead
And buried in life's mess.
Wherever I look I always see
The black ruins of my life,
Where I have spent so many years
Of withering and strife."

You will not find another land
You won't find other sea.
This town will always follow you
Wherever you may be.
You'll find that all localities
And streets are just the same.
As you grow old, every house
Will unchanged remain.
And do not hope to run away
From this neighbourhood –
Once you've ruined your life here.
It's nowhere any good.

The century of love and of creation

The century of love and of creation,
The century of recognition,
The century of never-ceasing beauty,
The times of values
And the times of fame,
The century of gratitude and love!

The pleasure from abundance
Of boundless inspiration,
The century of love and of creation –
Of peace and art and love!

02
MAY

26 MONDAY

27 TUESDAY

28 WEDNESDAY

29 THURSDAY

30 FRIDAY

01 SATURDAY

02 SUNDAY

AIYA MAXUTOVA (KAZAKHSTAN)

How many spring days I stood
At our village place,
And, fumbling with my scarf, I would
Wait to see your face.

That tiny green apple tree sprout
You planted long ago
Is now a bride coming out
With pearls as white as snow.

How many spring days I stood
At our village place,
And, fumbling with my scarf, I would
Wait to see your face.

03

MAY

My grandfather came to Berlin

My grandfather came to Berlin, making his way in the 41st.
Wrapped in gunpowder, smoke, he performed great deeds,
As is testified by the Order – the Order of the Red Star.
Konev – the Marshal of the Great Country – gave it to him personally.

A medal "For Courage" in the midst of the most terrible war.
It was thoroughly deserved - everyone was astounded by his action.
Alone, completely without support, cut off behind enemy lines,
With just a grenade he took the enemy headquarters and captured the 'living tongue'.

As a reward for his character, he earned the nickname:
Fedor Andreevich Corshun – that's what the whole village called him.
In Smelyzh, the partisan region, the people knew a lot of grief,
And they didn't just give such nicknames to anyone.

This is the first time, I've written about him, although Polevoy wrote too,
As he would not leave the lad alone and 'dragged' him all over the place.
He shared his soldiering, looked after him as a 'son of the regiment',
And in the postwar years took the place of his father at his wedding.

Konoplin reached Berlin and did not die in the war;
He died as a different kind of warrior in his Bryansk native land.
His grave is unknown; it is unknown who killed him.
It is known that day in court, he had fought as in battle …
And setting the whole truth without fear to the court.
The crash of wheels hid his last secret from us,
My grandfather got on the train, but the train didn't bring him …

Veterans are leaving us, and they're not around anymore,
Only in the Immortal Regiment their hearts will burn:
To think about us, the children, the grandchildren of the Great Country -
The country has been saved for us,
And we save the history.

04
MAY

All through his life he drew the scenes of war…"

All through his life he drew the scenes of war.
One starless night, he hit a mine at dawn
And travelled to the bottom with the ship,
His final picture incompletely drawn.
All through his life, they came to him for cures,
He fought a furious battle against death
And died, from self-injection of the plague,
Research unfinished at his final breath.
All through his life he tested planes — and hearts,
Beginning with the Neuport as a boy.
He crashed when he was forty, to the end
Not having tested out the final toy.
We simply cannot get into our minds
That people do not always die in bed.
They die abruptly, with unfinished work,
Before they reach the target, they are dead!
As if a lifetime's cares may reach an end,
A lifetime's tasks, and then a final one,
And then, amidst one's family, there's peace,
A chair and rest, old age and all is done.

Translated by Mike Munford

09

MAY

03 MONDAY

04 TUESDAY

05 WEDNESDAY

06 THURSDAY

07 FRIDAY

08 SATURDAY   **09 SUNDAY**

The star of honour

Once again, all are happy to see the parade,
A true symbol of the glorious canon;
A soldier with a child shines like an icon
Amid the constellation of medals laid.

It burns in the heart of the damascene blade
That slew the dragon with breath of fire;
And scarlet banners flutter from every spire,
Turning the city to a marvellous glade.

But who will heal the wounds of the heart,
The terrible memory of the veterans' part –
The cost of all those brave victories?

Yes, we are so proud of your bold red flag
That finally promised the world some ease
When raised to the top of the Reichstag,

10
MAY

The Immortal Regiment

For the Motherland – the cry rings clearly.
We cannot retreat – the truth is plain.
We pray to the Almighty to sustain
Us through this sharp knot in our destiny.

High above the cranes call sweet
As they leave the battle to soar away,
Saluting us. And their beauty stays
To inspire us to each new feat.

The foe's relentless and the guns roar.
We are ready lie beneath the tanks.
But we'll vanquish evil with holy tears.

A Great Victory is our stronghold sure,
And triumph will ever be sung with thanks
To the Immortal Regiment that conquered fears!

12
MAY

PEDRO BONIFACIO PALACIOS (ARGENTINA)

Lo que yo quiero

Quiero ser las dos niñas de tus ojos,
las metálicas cuerdas de tu voz,
el rubor de tu sien cuando meditas
y el origen tenaz de tu rubor.

Quiero ser esas manos invisibles
que manejan por sí la Creación,
y formar con tus sueños y los míos
otro mundo mejor para los dos.

Eres tú, providencia de mi vida,
mi sostén, mi refugio, mi caudal:
cual si fueras mi madre yo te amo…
¡y todavía más!

I WANT TO BE

I want to be the girls of both your eyes,
The string of your voice when you speak,
I want to be the rose blush on your cheeks,
The blush that brings colour to your skin.

I want to be those invisible hands
That make the world go round,
And shape it with our dreams,
both yours and mine,
To make the world better for us.

Yes, it is you: my life's guiding light,
My support, my refuge, my fate.
I love you as a child loves a mother…
And many, many times more!

13

MAY

Overall, I am deeply suspicious of Impressionism. As a 19th-century movement in the Arts, it seems to be continually dominated by inconsequential compositions, with far too much emphasis on our ever-changing perspectives - exaggerated, as these occasionally are, by the effects of one's passage through time. This is not to say, of course, that only empirical facts should be the defining feature of aesthetic endeavour. Indeed, the predictably dreary and often bland productions of Soviet-style Social Realism perpetually stand as a grim reminder to this failing. However, "abstraction", in itself, obviously stretches beyond an insistence on arbitrary sensory adjustments, inordinately detailed atmospheres, or evocative environmental qualities. Truly, our world makes an impression upon the physical senses, but as part of a two-way process; whereby human exteriors struggle against an equal flood of sophisticated substances welling up from inside ourselves. So, editing a series of manifestly Impressionist poems by Lenar Shayeh in his collection *One of You* was, at first, something of a mixed blessing.

ISBN: 978-1-910886-47-2
RRP: £9.50

15

MAY

TO VLADA, A SONNET

Oh my dear Vlada, do I think of you at all?
You should ask a heart, can it ever rest?
Or tireless Earth cease spinning from the west?
Or the high Moon, if it's about to fall?
I think of you from the time I wake
As dawn's grey light spreads softly on my bed
And through the busy day you're in my head
Through all the routine daily give and take.
And when at last it's time for me to sleep
I close my eyes and still you're here with me.
You're in my thoughts and will ever be
You're always there, of course – there to keep!
But there's one question, I think you must agree:
Tell me, dearest, do you ever think of me?

16

MAY

10 MONDAY

11 TUESDAY

12 WEDNESDAY

13 THURSDAY

14 FRIDAY

15 SATURDAY   16 SUNDAY

*"Day of Remembrance
for Victims of Deportation
of the Crimean Tatar People
May 18, 1944"*

**18
MAY**

MEMORIES OF MY FATHER

The executioner held the fate of Tatars.
We were taken from our homes by trains.
One day we halted under the stars
And heard the haunting call of the cranes.

Anxious, desperate, far away.
They cry aloud for sympathy.
For heaven's aid, they sadly pray
But the Earth is weeping silently.

I wanted to fly away on wings
And I prayed to the Lord to answer me –
Tears rollng down, and whispering
The words in my heart unstoppably.

How can the birds with their pure hearts
Understand the folk down here?
When your day as executioner starts
With women, the old, and children dear.

P.S.

In spring, swallows dart under the eaves again.
But father never returned to Crimea
And if I ever hear the cry of a crane
My heart shrinks and I shed many a tear…

THE MAID OF TORO

O, low shone the sun on the fair lake of Toro,
And weak were the whispers that waved the dark wood,
All as a fair maiden, bewilder'd in sorrow,
Sorely sigh'd to the breezes, and wept to the flood.
"O, saints! from the mansions of bliss lowly bending;
Now grant my petition, in anguish ascending,
My Henry restore, or let Eleanor die!"

All distant and faint were the sounds of the battle,
With the breezes they rise, with the breezes they fail,
Till the shout, and the groan, and the conflict's dread rattle,
And the chase's wild clamour, came loading the gale.
Breathless she gazed on the woodlands so dreary;
Slowly approaching a warrior was seen;
Life's ebbing tide mark'd his footsteps so weary,
Cleft was his helmet, and woe was his mien.

"O, save thee, fair maid, for our armies are flying!
O, save thee, fair maid, for thy guardian is low!
Deadly cold on yon heath thy brave Henry is lying,
Scarce could he falter the tidings of sorrow,
And scarce could she hear them, benumb'd with despair:
And when the sun sunk on the sweet lake of Toro,
For ever he set to the Brave and the Fair.

22

MAY

Гу́нён Торо (DUNGAN)

Торо даху́ тянбянди, луэвэ жуэвандыйли.
Фын щёншын зэ фулин, манмар нанвындыйли.
Гу́нён пэфанди, чинжё фын, чинжё филю -
нянлуй тонди бу тынли.
Тянтонниди жу́минду, ба вэ ниму тинжянни.
Ба Данын яндин ду чито, ги та фанчон нэлянни.
Ба Генри! Ги вэ туйги… Гу́нён Мария!
Ба тади мин, ни жюха, булиму, Линор е сыни.

Дажонди жүнчиди да щёншын, фынфыр гуади долэли.Лихэ
дуйтуди бинйүнму, доли вэму гынчянли.
Гонте дади гэзышын, вэму дажя тинжянли.
Жыма, зущён саду нанвынли.
Кэ йижынзы вэ тинди-таму дашын гощинли.
Да йүанчур гу́нён канжянли дэшонди жүнбин зубудунли.
Фулин бянни та канди, пэфан жүнбин дуанчидини.
Тушонди темозы канкэдини.

Куэщер гу́нён, жюминчи, лихэ дуйту лэдыйли.
Замуди жүнбин донбучу́ли.
Дэшон Генри дуннинли, нянжин йибыйзы зынбукэли.
Да фулин лэди дабэля, ба вэму дажя дабэли.
Фибянни гу́нён бэщинди, мэю щинчин, мэ жинли.
Жэту, Торо ху́ шонмяр, хи мамарди бу жянли.
Йинщүн жуйи, жүнмый зохуа йибыйзы таму канбужянли.

17 MONDAY

18 TUESDAY

19 WEDNESDAY

20 THURSDAY

21 FRIDAY

22 SATURDAY   23 SUNDAY

IVAN FRANKO (UKRAINE)

***

До моря сліз, під тиском пересудів
Пролитих, і моя вплила краплина;
До храму людських змагань, праць і трудів,
Чень, і моя доложиться цеглина.

А як мільйонів куплений сльозами
День світла, щастя й волі засвітає,
То, чень, в новім, великім людськім храмі
Хтось добрим словом і мене згадає.

28

MAY

***

Into the sea of tears, swept by the pain of life,
I shed a drop of my own hard tears.
And in the temple of human work and strife,
I lay my own brick of sweat and fears.

And when it is bought by millions of tears,
A new day dawns – of light and joy when all are free –
Then if that new and greater temple nears
Someone may kindly remember me.

29
MAY

HAMID LARBI (FRANCE)

Glance of exile

The spirit of pains
Startling in shadows of memories
The isolated allegory on speechless walls
Each wall filled with ordeal

Wounded consideration
Of evasive voices
And in the glance of exile
Deep silence

Words unspoken
Lives destroyed by a Creator without effigy
Who creates and afterwards gives up
He doesn't plead for his offence
Ceaseless sorrow prevails

Hollowing out in the mind:
Where do sails go below the horizon?
To be erected by the relief
Or the rain blown by the wind?
The mind engulfed in darkness
Up till logic stops vibrating.

30

MAY

24 MONDAY

25 TUESDAY

26 WEDNESDAY

27 THURSDAY

28 FRIDAY

29 SATURDAY   30 SUNDAY

Rusalka

Down by the lake, where dark trees grow thick,
Lived a monk who hoped to be saved.
He drove himself on with the sternest of sticks;
He fasted, he prayed and he slaved.
As he laboured away with his humble spade,
He was digging his grave with each breath.
To the Saints every day, he earnestly prayed
To release him from life into death.

Then one summer's day, as he kneeled by the stairs
At the door of his tumbledown shack,
This anchorite gave the good Lord his prayers.
The forest began to grow black.
A mist over the lake like smoke did arise
And a blood-red moon rose from its sleep
To roll along slowly, through churning skies.
The monk gazed on the waters so deep.

As he looks and he looks, his mind fills with fear;
He can't understand what he's thinking...
But he sees all too clear, water bubbling near
Then all at once quietly sinking...
And suddenly there, white as first snows,
Pale as the shadows of night,
A naked girl from the waters arose
And emerges silent and bright.

She stares at the monk as she sits by the lake
And softly combs her wet hair.
The holy old monk, in fear starts to shake,
Entranced by her beauty so fair.

01

JUNE

She beckons him on with a wave of her hand
And nods to him quickly, come to me.
Then like a falling star she's gone from the land
To plunge in the waters so gloomy.

All that long night, the old man can't sleep
All the long day, he can't pray.
His mind is filled with the girl from the deep;
Her loveliness won't go away.
Then once again, the woods dress in night,
The moon starts to redden once more
And there in full view, so lovely and bright,
Sits the naked girl down by the shore.

She nods to the monk with so teasing a gaze –
Blows kisses to him, sweet and wild.
And like summer waves, she splashes and plays,
And laughs and cries like a child.
Then tenderly moaning, she calls to the monk,
"Monk! Monk! Come to me! Come to me!"
Then into the lake, in a trice, now she's sunk;
Silence reigns again under the trees.

On the third day, by the enchanted shore,
Sat the passion-filled old anchorite
To wait for the maid, lovely as before,
And the woods filled with shadows of night...
When bright dawn came up and kicked out the night,
The monk was nowhere to be seen,
But some boys passing by said they caught sight
Of a beard, afloat on the waters so green.

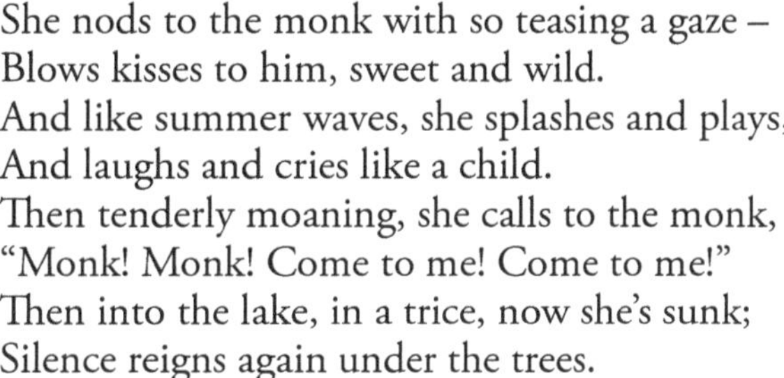

Paisaje

La tarde equivocada
se vistió de frío.
Detrás de los cristales,
turbios, todos los niños,
ven convertirse en pájaros
un árbol amarillo.

La tarde está tendida
a lo largo del río.
Y un rubor de manzana
tiembla en los tejadillos.

Scenery

The afternoon's dressed in cold,
The wind shivers.
Behind the windows
Children watch
How yellow leaves
Turn into birds and fly away.

The afternoon is resting
Down by the river.
The apple blush
Trembles on the veranda.

06

JUNE

31 MONDAY

01 TUESDAY

02 WEDNESDAY

03 THURSDAY

04 FRIDAY

05 SATURDAY

06 SUNDAY

LULLABY OF AN INFANT CHIEF

Oh, hush thee, my babie, thy sire was a knight,
Thy mother, a lady, both lovely and bright;
The woods and the glens, from the towers which we see,
They all are belonging, dear babie, to thee.

Oh, fear not the bugle, though loudly it blows,
It calls but the warders that guard thy repose;
Their bows would be bended, their blades would be red,
Ere the step of a foeman draws near to thy bed.

Oh, hush thee, my babie, the time will soon come,
When thy sleep shall be broken by trumpet and drum
Then hush thee, my darling, take rest while you may,
For strife comes with manhood, and waking with day.

10

JUNE

СПИ, ДИТИНОНЬКО (UKRAINIAN)

Спи, дитинонько, спи та зростай, мов сокіл!
Батько твій був народним героєм,
Твоя мати — краса чарувала окіл,—
Вічна пам'ять їм з тихим покоєм!

Спи, дитинонько, спи та зростай, мов сокіл!
Все дістанеш: і ниви, і луки;
Боронити твій сон у нас вистачить сил;
Чуєш: сурм розлягаються гуки?

Спи, дитинонько, спи! А підійде черга:
Сам дружини направиш до бою,
Бо час бою на смерть, лихий час настига,
День визволу веде за собою.

Translation
by Pavlo Grabovskiy, 1897

Mar Português

Ó mar salgado, quanto do teu sal
São lágrimas de Portugal!
Por te cruzarmos, quantas mães choraram,
Quantos filhos em vão rezaram!
Quantas noivas ficaram por casar
Para que fosses nosso, ó mar!

Valeu a pena? Tudo vale a pena
Se a alma não é pequena.
Quem quer passar além do Bojador
Tem que passar além da dor.
Deus ao mar o perigo e o abismo deu,
Mas nele é que espelhou o céu.

The Sea of Portugal

O salty sea, how much of your salt
Is the sad tears of Portugal?
How many mothers cried for you,
How many children prayed hopelessly,
How many unwed brides for you,
That you should be ours, oh sea?

Was it worth it? Yes, worth it all
If your soul is true and not small.
If you desire to go past Bojador
You must go beyond pain and more.
God gave the sea dangers, depths to defy,
And coloured it blue to mirror the sky.

13

JUNE

07 MONDAY

08 TUESDAY

09 WEDNESDAY

10 THURSDAY

11 FRIDAY

12 SATURDAY   13 SUNDAY

Peste vârfuri

Peste vârfuri trece lună,
Codru-şi bate frunza lin,
Dintre ramuri de arin
Melancolic cornul sună.

Mai departe, mai departe,
Mai încet, tot mai încet,
Sufletu-mi nemângâiet
Îndulcind cu dor de moarte.

De ce taci, când fermecată
Inima-mi spre tine-ntorn?
Mai suna-vei, dulce corn,
Pentru mine vreodată?

15

JUNE

Over Peaks

The moon is rising over the heights,
Striking the forest leaves so softly,
The horn is calling oh so sadly,
Among the alder trees this night.

It's going, going, going away,
It's slowing, slowing, slowing,
And my soul is comforted in knowing
The sweet longing for death today.

Why have you fallen silent as dew
When you stole my heart away?
Come again, sweet horn, and play –
Play for me forever, won't you?

16
JUNE

MY PERFECT PARTNER

Oh my perfect partner, dance through the world with me
Let's whirl across life's dance floor, let our steps be free!
I may not have much technique; my feet are made of clay;
My legs are made of jelly and my rhythm's all astray.
But my love is more than ready to sweep you off your feet:
To glide and swoop precisely and match you beat for beat.
My heart will dance your polka, my words will be your rond
And as we move together, our love will be our bond.
Our ballroom's in the land of dreams, not stuck upon the floor.
Our waltz can glide on skywards and last forever more.
And if you think my chasse is wobbly now and then,
When it comes to final scoring, my love's a perfect ten!

20

JUNE

14 MONDAY

15 TUESDAY

16 WEDNESDAY

17 THURSDAY

18 FRIDAY

19 SATURDAY   20 SUNDAY

Dedicated to all soldiers, former and present combatants and military re-enactors

You're marching in columns, like serpents, holding banners high,
With flintlocks or swords of steel, you are striding by,
Or raising your rifles, confronting the savage foe…
Yet so many of you are leaving, too many, even so.

You're arrayed along the border where it's crossed with firestorm,
Protected by your helmets, united by uniform.
But none of you is lost, or forgotten, or deprived of fame -
For the duty of a woman is remembering every name.

As I remember, we all do – no one is forgotten.
In the forests of rifles, among tunics of cotton,
In the soldier hundreds traversing the murky mire –
I'm looking at you. Every moment. And I aspire.

My gaze is not armour, nor shield, and it cannot be.
Those deaths in early summer are terrible to see…
They fall down. Their coats and their faces are waxen-pale.
The sprouts are growing now through them in the battle-dale.

Stand up! I appeal, and I believe it's true.
Stand up! Many years you have to live and will go by for you.
Stand up! All the bullets are shot, and so few of them pass…

But you raise your hands, and you fall,
dead,
down into the grass.

21

JUNE

***

Вражда меж стран, вражда в крови,
Но все мы часть одной Земли,
Но все мы часть одной Любви,
На распрях семьи обрели.

Вражда за дом, вражда за клан,
Но Дом Земной нам Богом дан,
На всех один язык любви,
Где вдохновение в крови.

Вражда, как сон, сквозь океан,
Сильнее люди мирных стран,
Но сила в мудрости, в крови,
Пусть будет Эра для Любви…

***

Strife's in the world, in blood runs strife,
But we are parts of Earth – one life.
We're parts of Love, a single core,
We built our families on discord.

Strife for our home, strife for our clan,
But God gave Earthly Home to man.
Language of love for all is one,
While inspiration in blood runs.

Strife like night's sleep goes through the sea.
The strongest live in lands of peace;
Strength is in blood. Strength of a sage,
Let Love give rise to a new Age…

22
JUNE

This book is a bilingual collection by a **Belarusian award-winning poet Anna Komar**. The poems in the book are strongly personal, yet they are reflections of the reality that is so familiar to many of us. Love, friendship, self-exploration, childhood memories, fears – Anna finds new ways to speak about the things we have heard so much about, and her voice is frank. The thread connecting the poems in this collection is being a woman in the strongly patriarchal society which Belarus still is. These poems are a rebellion, they touch, provoke, embarrass, get under your skin, but leave hope that the wounds will be healed, the home will be found, and love will live in it.

ISBN: 978-1-910886-81-6
RRP: £20.50

27

JUNE

21 MONDAY

22 TUESDAY

23 WEDNESDAY

24 THURSDAY

25 FRIDAY

26 SATURDAY   27 SUNDAY

Prof. Viačaslaŭ Rahojša Minsk
A POETIC TREASURY FROM BELARUS

А хто там ідзе?

А хто там ідзе, а хто там ідзе
У агромністай такой грамадзе? — Беларусы.
А што яны нясуць на худых плячах, На руках у крыві, на нагах
у лапцях? — Сваю крыўду.
А куды ж нясуць гэту крыўду ўсю, А куды ж нясуць напаказ
сваю? — На свет цэлы.
А хто гэта іх, не адзін мільён,
Крыўду несць наўчыў, разбудзіў іх сон? — Бяда, гора.
А чаго ж, чаго захацелась ім,
Пагарджаным век, ім, сляпым, глухім? — Людзьмі звацца.

1905—1907

And, say, who goes there?

And, say, who goes there? And, say, who goes there?
In such a mighty throng assembled, O declare! Belarusians!
And what do those lean shoulders bear as load,
Those hands stained dark with blood,
those feet bast-sandal shod?
All their grievance!
And to what place do they this grievance bear,
And whither do they take it to declare?
To the whole world!
And who schooled them thus, many million strong,
Bear their grievance forth,
roused them from slumbers long?
Want and suffering!
And what is it, then, for which so long they pined,
Scorned throughout the years, they, the deaf, the blind? To be called human!

Translated by Vera Rich

29
JUNE

Лето

Тянулось в жажде к хоботкам
И бабочкам и пятнам,
Обоим память оботкав
Медовым, майным, мятным.
Не ход часов, но звон цепов
С восхода до захода
Вонзался в воздух сном шипов,
Заворожив погоду.
Бывало — нагулявшись всласть,
Закат сдавал цикадам
И звездам и деревьям власть
Над кухнею и садом.
Не тени — балки месяц клал,
А то бывал в отлучке,
И тихо, тихо ночь текла
Трусцой, от тучки к тучке.
Скорей со сна, чем с крыш; скорей
Забывчивый, чем робкий,
Топтался дождик у дверей,
И пахло винной пробкой.
Так пахла пыль. Так пах бурьян.
И, если разобраться,
Так пахли прописи дворян
О равенстве и братстве.
Вводили земство в волостях,
С другими — вы, не так ли?
Дни висли, в кислице блестя,
И винной пробкой пахли.

1917

Summer

Athirst for insects, butterflies.
And stains we long had waited,
And round us both were memories
Of heat, mint, honey plaited.
No clocks chimed, but the flail rang clear
From dawn to dusk and planted
Its dreams of stings into the air.
The weather was enchanted.
Strolled sunset to its heart's content,
They yielded to cicadas
And stars and trees its government
Of gardens and of larders.
The moon in absence, out of sight.
Not shade but baulks was throwing.
And softly, softly the shy night
From cloud to cloud was flowing.
From dream more than from roof, and more
Forgetful than faint-hearted.
Soft rain was shuffling at the door
And smell of wine-corks spurted.
So smelt the dust. So smelt the grass
And if we chanced to heed them.
Smell from the gentry's teaching was
Of brotherhood and freedom.
The councils met in villages;
Weren't you with those that held them?
Bright with wood-sorrel hung the days,
And smell of wine-corks filled them.

*Translated
by Cecil Maurice Bowra*

YULIA PUCHKOVA (RUSSIA)

You See it in My Eyes

You see it in my eyes,
I see in yours,
But there is nothing we can do about it.
What I consider blessed,
You call cursed,
And there is no one in between to doubt it.

The more we live, the more apart we are –
Two banks of flesh divided with a scar
That never heals, the pain is never-ending –
Misunderstanding.

A Vessel

Look in the brain and you will find wires,
Look in the heart and you will find blood.
Wherever there's a vessel of desires
That tend from time to time to overflood
The brain, the heart, no doubt it isn't here –
It's out of the body and this world.
There is a single thing I really fear:
When they do find the vessel far or near,
They'll definitely claim they've found God.

03

JULY

28 MONDAY

29 TUESDAY

30 WEDNESDAY

01 THURSDAY

02 FRIDAY

03 SATURDAY   04 SUNDAY

I'm not an enchantress.

You called me your enchantress.
I'm embarrassed to keep on listening,
I simply write poems on moonless nights
About my love and my king.

I'm not an enchantress, so what?
Like you, I'm an earthly being,
I'm no friend of Devil or God;
I just draw the fine dreams I'm seeing.

Some sudden whim comes and hits me
And I'm mad with longing for you.
What a shame that you're not in Paris,
Where love greets the morning dew.

05

JULY

Kada manęs nebus

Kalnuos laisvi ereliai nardo,-
Kalnuos ir mes abu—
Vai, kas kartos tau mano varda
Kada kalnų nebus?

Mums vejas laisves dainą suokia.
Laisviem nerūpi nieks!
Vai, kas primins tau mano juoką,
Kai vasara prabėgs?

Diena su saule nusileido,-
Su saule vėl nubus—
Vai, kai pakeiks tau mano meilę,
Kada manęs nebus?

06
JULY

WHEN I'M GONE

The eagles are in the mountains.
We are between them too.
But who'll repeat my name to you,
When no mountains do?

The wind fills all the world with songs.
What ails you wind, do say!
Who will remind you of my laugh,
When summer goes away?

The Sun will put each day to sleep
And wake it up again.
But tell me who can go as deep
As goes my love, my friend?

Translated by
Tatiana Vasilieva

05 MONDAY

06 TUESDAY

07 WEDNESDAY

08 THURSDAY

09 FRIDAY

10 SATURDAY

11 SUNDAY

**QUENTIN DURWARD
CHAPTER XIV: THE JOURNEY**

I see thee yet, fair France—thou favour'd land
Of art and nature—thou art still before me,
Thy sons, to whom their labour is a sport,
So well thy grateful soil returns its tribute,
Thy sunburnt daughters, with their laughing eyes
And glossy raven locks. But, favour'd France,
Thou hast had many a tale of woe to tell
In ancient times as now.

ANONYMOUS

CHAPTER XV: THE GUIDE

He was a son of Egypt, as he told me,
And one descended from those dread magicians,
Who waged rash war, when Israel dwelt in Goshen,
With Israel and her Prophet—matching rod
With his, the son's of Levi's—and encountering
Jehovah's miracles with incantations,
Till upon Egypt came the avenging Angel,
And those proud sages wept for their first born,
As wept the unletter'd peasant.

ANONYMOUS

12

JULY

QVENTIN DURWARD (FINNISH)
XIV MATKUSTUS

Sun näen vielä, Ranska ihana,
sä luonnon sekä taiteen suosituinen,
nään poikas, joille työ on huvitusta –
niin runsaan veron suopi aulis maa;
nään tyttäresi, päivän rusoittamat,
veitikkasilmät, korpinkarva-hiukset.
Vaan kuitenkin sä, Ranska suosittu,
jo olet nähnyt monta surua
niin muinoin kuin myös nytkin.

NIMETÖN.

XV OPAS

"Min' olen" niin hän virkkoi mulle, "maalta
Egyptin, tuota noitasukua,
mi, koska Gosenissa asui Israel,
hurjasti ryhtyi taisteluhun vastaan
Mosesta sekä kansaa Moseksen,
Jehovan ihmetöitä vastustaen
omilla loitsukonsteillaan, siks kunnes
lähestyi koston enkeli ja viisaat
kopeat esikoisiaan sai surra
kuin oppimaton talonpoikakin.

NIMETÖN.

*Translation
by Julius Krohn 1917*

13
JULY

Sonnet 18: Shall I compare the to a summer's day?

Shall I compare the to a summer's day?
Thou art more lovely and more temperate.
Rough winds do shake the darling buds of May,
And summer's lease hath all too short a date.
Sometime too hot the eye of heaven shines,
And often is his gold complexion dimmed;
And every fair from fair sometime declines,
By chance, or nature's changing course, untrimmed;
But thy eternal summer shall not fade,
Nor lose possession of that fair thou ow'st,
Nor shall death brag thou wand'rest in his shade,
When in eternal lines to Time thou grow'st.
    So long as men can breathe, or eyes can see,
    So long lives this, and this gives life to thee.

14
JULY

12 MONDAY

13 TUESDAY

14 WEDNESDAY

15 THURSDAY

16 FRIDAY

17 SATURDAY   18 SUNDAY

THE BAREFOOTED FRIAR (From Ivanhoe)

I'll give thee, good fellow, a twelvemonth or twain,
To search Europe through, from Byzantium to Spain;
But ne'er shall you find, should you search till you tire,
So happy a man as the Barefooted Friar.

Your knight for his lady pricks forth in career,
And is brought home at even-song bunny'd through with a spear;
I confess him in haste - for his lady desires
No comfort on earth save the Barefooted Friar's.

Your monarch? - Pshaw! many a prince has been known
To barter his robes for our cowl and our gown,
But which of us e'er felt the idle desire
To exchange for a crown the grey hood of a Friar!

The Friar has walk'd out, and where'er he has gone,
The land and its fatness is mark'd for his own;
He can roam where he lists, he can stop when he tires,
For every man's house is the Barefooted Friar's.

He's expected at noon, and no wight till he comes
May profane the great chair, or the porridge of plums
For the best of the cheer, and the seat by the fire,
Is the undenied right of the Barefooted Friar.

He's expected at night, and the pasty's made hot,
They broach the brown ale, and they fill the black pot,
And the goodwife would wish the goodman in the mire,
Ere he lack'd a soft pillow, the Barefooted Friar.

19
JULY

Le carme déchaussé (FRENCH)

Je te donnerai, bonhomme, une année ou deux
Pour chercher à travers l'Europe, depuis l'Espagne jusqu'à Byzance,
Et tu ne trouveras jamais, quelque étendue que soit la revue,
Un homme aussi heureux que le carme déchaussé.

Le chevalier se lance dans la carrière pour sa dame,
Et, le soir, on le ramène à la maison blessé.
Je le confesse en hâte, sa dame ne désire
Aucune consolation sur la terre, sauf celle du carme déchaussé.

Le monarque, bah ! le prince a été connu
Pour avoir changé sa robe contre le froc et le capuchon ;
Mais lequel d'entre nous a jamais eu le vain désir
De troquer contre une couronne le capuchon gris du carme déchaussé.

Le carme est sorti, et partout où il est allé
Il a trouvé bon accueil et bon gîte.
Il peut errer où il veut, il peut s'arrêter quand il est las,
Car la maison de chacun est ouverte au carme déchaussé.

On l'attend à midi, et aucun rustre, jusqu'à ce qu'il arrive,
Ne peut profaner la stalle ou la soupe aux pruneaux,
Car la meilleure chère et la place près du feu
Sont le droit incontestable du carme déchaussé.

Le soir, on l'attend et l'on chauffe le pâté,
On ouvre le tonneau d'ale brune et on emplit le pot noir,
Et la brune femme souhaiterait son mari dans la cave,
Plutôt qu'il manquât un doux lit au carme déchaussé.

*Translation by
Alexandre Dumas
XIX*

20
JULY

IVAN VAZOV (BULGARIA)

Към природата - откъс

Не си ли ти отзив на мъдрост всезнайна,
творенье гигантско на мощна ръка?
Не е ли в теб видна таз личност нам тайна?
Не е ли вплътена в теб, тъй да река?

Не всуе човекът лишен от лъчите
на светлий източник, с дух немощен, слаб,
от толкоз величье ударен в очите,
божил те, кланял се, мислил се твой раб.

Поети, теб чеда любими, щастливи,
кои си дарила с най-редкий си дар,
не в тебе ли черпят тез мисли светливи?
Не ти ли им вдъхваш тез песни и жар?

Най-сетне в теб само, във твойте прегръдки
нетленни и драги, о, майко света,
духът ни отруден от светските мъки
намира утеха, покой, радостта!

To Nature – Excerp

Are you not a reflection of an omniscient mind,
The vast creation of a powerful hand?
Although we can never see the figure behind,
Isn't it embodied in you - do you understand?

No, it's not for nothing that Man is so poor.
Deprived of the light, his spirit is frail.
Seeing such glory he bowed low before you
He worshipped you and gave himself without fail.

Do not poets, your most beloved offspring –
Those who you gave a gift of such worth –
Draw on you for their thoughts, their lyrics inspir-
ing?
Don't you fill up their songs with warmth?

O Mother, only in your warm embrace
Can the weary heart of your poor little boy,
Who's tired of life and the world and its race,
Find comfort and peace, inspiration and joy!

23

JULY

19 MONDAY

20 TUESDAY

21 WEDNESDAY

22 THURSDAY

23 FRIDAY

24 SATURDAY   25 SUNDAY

Ivanhoe CHAPTER XL

Knight.

Anna-Marie, love, up is the sun,
Anna-Marie, love, morn is begun,
Mists are dispersing, love, birds singing free,
Up in the morning, love, Anna-Marie.
Anna-Marie, love, up in the morn,
The hunter is winding blithe sounds on his horn,
The echo rings merry from rock and from tree,
'Tis time to arouse thee, love, Anna-Marie.

Wamba.

O Tybalt, love, Tybalt, awake me not yet,
Around my soft pillow while softer dreams flit,
For what are the joys that in waking we prove,
Compared with these visions, O, Tybalt, my love?
Let the birds to the rise of the mist carol shrill,
Let the hunter blow out his loud horn on the hill,
Softer sounds, softer pleasures, in slumber I prove,---
But think not I dreamt of thee, Tybalt, my love.

26
JULY

Ivanhoe, XL peatükk (ESTONIAN)

Rüütel.

Anna-Marie, päikese tõus,
Anna-Marie, hommik on jõus,
Udu on lahkumas, lindude laul,
Ärka, oh armas, hommiku aul!
Anna-Marie, hommikuga
Ju jahimees tuututab pasunaga
Ja vastu tal kajamas kalju ning laan,
Käes silmapilk, kus ma su äratan.

Wamba.

Oh Tybalt, mu Tybalt, ä'ä ärata veel,
Sest unede padjul mul aelemas meel,
Ei päevaseid rõõmusid võrrelda või
Ma nendega, mis mulle unehõlm tõi.
Las linnuke tõusta ja lõõritada,
Las jahimees sarvega tuututada,
Ma unes küll paremat maitseda saan.
Mu Tybalt, ä'ä usu, et s'ust unistan.

*Translation by A. H.
Tammsaare, 1926*

27

JULY

The Eagle

No quarry escapes the trained eagle's blow
Yet some saps still keep a poor kestrel or crow.
And when the genuine hunter's set free to fly,
These rank amateurs also let their pets go!
And so the crows croak croak in the air far below
And the kestrels squeal squeal higher up, and oh
On and on they cry – so the eagle's denied.
They fly all through the day, but there's nothing to show.
Yet the owners smile smile as if nothing's awry
And none thinks to question this meaningless show,
Or ask what it is they've got from the sky.
They just brag on all night; they caw and they crow.
There's no good for the soul, no peace to come by.
Well – this is all the poor people know.

01
AUGUST

26 MONDAY

27 TUESDAY

28 WEDNESDAY

29 THURSDAY

30 FRIDAY

31 SATURDAY

01 SUNDAY

HAMID LARBI (FRANCE)

The Humanities

Anxiety, agony and hope
Examining the idea within the inner self
An enlightened idea, an insignificant idea
That follows the mind

To be immersed so many times
To be amazed, to be furious
Travelling aimlessly through the Humanities
In the absence of light

It is there, face to face
A dialogue goes on in solitude
Observing it
And ending up stripped unveiled

Nasty appearances
Whisper of melodious ideas
And furtive tunes crossing the mind
An inner call to close the eyes
And sense
Where to travel.

04
AUGUST

THE TROUBADOUR

Glowing with love, on fire for fame
A Troubadour that hated sorrow
Beneath his lady's window came,
And thus he sung his last good-morrow:
"My arm it is my country's right,
My heart is in my true-love's bower;
Gaily for love and fame to fight
Befits the gallant Troubadour."

And while he marched with helm on head
And harp in hand, the descant rung,
As faithful to his favourite maid,
The minstrel-burden still he sung:
"My arm it is my country's right,
My heart is in my lady's bower;
Resolved for love and fame to fight
I come, a gallant Troubadour."

07
AUGUST

Troubadour (CZECH)

Pln lásky, dychtiv po slávě
kýs' troubadour, jenž neznal péčí,
ku dámy svojí oslavě
jí před okny své „s bohem" vděčí:
„Má páž mé vlasti vzdána jest,
však srdce touží k paní vzhůru,
tak v boj jdu za lásku a čest,
jak ctnému sluší troubadouru."

Když s štítem spěl a přilbicí
a s harfou v ruce z brány hradu,
své krásné věren dívčici
si hlasně zpíval do úpadu:
„Má páž mé vlasti vzdána jest,
však srdce k paní touží vzhůru,
tak v boj jdu za lásku a čest,
jak ctnému sluší troubadouru."

Translation
by Jaroslav Vrchlický, 1900

02 MONDAY

03 TUESDAY

04 WEDNESDAY

05 THURSDAY

06 FRIDAY

07 SATURDAY   08 SUNDAY

The Nation

Oh my luckless Kazakh, my unfortunate kin,
An unkempt moustache hides your mouth and chin.
Blood on your right cheek, fat on your left —
When will the dawn of your reason begin?

Your looks are not bad and your numbers are vast,
Yet why do you change your favours so fast?
You will never listen to sound advice,
Your tongue in its rashness is unsurpassed. (…)

Kinsmen for trifle each other hate.
God bereft them of reason — such is their fate.
No honor, no harmony, only dissent;
No wonder cattle is scarcer of late.

Translation by Dorian Rottenberg

The title of Anastasiya Kuzmicheva's work *"Belarusian Whales"* invites readers into a world of contradictions and doubts. Indeed, while reading these verses one grasps the apparently conflicting depths of the author's own point of view - thanks to a wide and clever usage of poetic figures. As such, her sky is "always without make-up", while her brain "will wipe the dream like dust". Meanwhile, warmth, light, shame, and love, are created through the imagery surrounding a "white temple" ….. an antithesis to previous assertions. Overall, this poet's irony seems to be both subtle and comical, since one encounters lines like: "a whale escaped like all men" as a clear critique of average truth claims. Hence, those parts of the poem devoted to meaningful answers and pithy solutions remains the largest section of the entire composition. Albeit quickly followed by more questions. Curiously, neither "who", nor "what" the whales represent is ever outlined. Instead, a sense of intelligent mystery points to "the names of chapters" as our only clue. After all, we already know that " …everyone saw the whale…", which leaves each reader to make up his, or her, own mind in this regard.

— *Nadezhda Kolesnikova, writer*

ISBN: 978-1-910886-45-8
RRP: £14.95

11
AUGUST

In this bold and insightful second collection of Neo-Expressionist literatures, Raushan Burkit Bayeva-Nukenova invites her readers to revel in the cogitations of a Kazakh Radical Traditionalist. A literary position provoking the exploration of Eurasian motives, Central Asian reactions to London, nomadic love, and the contours of ethnic memory. Each one of which is lyrically scrutinized - along with the dissonant place of women in our postmodern world. Indeed, unlike her highly successful and probing first volume The Wormwood Wind, the author of this present book seeks to extend her poetic analysis of current affairs, before taking her first tentative footsteps into prose. This may be why pundits are already saying that several diverse strains of autobiographical text stream throughout this fresh and innovative work. All explaining, of course, the obvious value of such a tome as a unique contribution to those literary discernments mapping contemporary femininities exact boundaries. Unarguably, therefore, Raushan Burkit Bayeva-Nukenova's examination of nationality, colour, religion, and cultural backgrounds, will both challenge the assumptions of Western readers, while opening the doors of perception into a uniquely Central Asian perspective.

ISBN: 978-1-910886-32-8
RRP: £19.95

15

AUGUST

09 MONDAY

10 TUESDAY

11 WEDNESDAY

12 THURSDAY

13 FRIDAY

14 SATURDAY   15 SUNDAY

***

Бегущему сквозь пагубную тьму
под грохот слухового водопада
по улицам уснувшего Карлсбада.

Невнятная, безумна речь его,
бегущего в ночи – ни для чего,
схватившего и сжавшего в кулак
пространство, измельченное во прах.

Его из этой бури не изъять:
там молнии скрутились в рукоять
гигантского, как смерч, коловорота.
В таких мирах для смертных нету брода.

Ночную мглу таранит глыба лба.
Сквозь молний шаровые колоба,
сквозь кожаные плети мощных струй,
гоним планидой, как солдат сквозь строй.

Промок зеленый ношенный сюртук.
Еще чуть-чуть и он услышит звук!
Вот грохот, шквал, потоп, обвал, облом...
Апплодисменты грянули, как гром.

О, просыпайся! И рукоплещи
Бетховену, бегущему в нощи.

Pity Beethoven – as he, grim-faced,
Through the vile and dark night raced.
Heedless of the waters' roar,
Through Carlsbad's sleeping streets he tore.

His speech was slurred and not quite sane.
He sped on through the gloom. In vain,
He clutched the air and clenched his fist
To crush to nought the damp night mist.

The awful storm brooks no escape.
The lightning twists into the shape
Of a vast tornado's maw –
No mortal can pass through this war.

Cold rain rams his massive brow.
Balls of lightning hunt him now.
Sharp whips of wind about him lay.
Fate drives him on; he must obey.

His green frock-coat is soaking wet.
But he cannot hear it yet!
The crash, the floods, land going under...
And then the booming claps of thunder.

Oh yes, wake up, and clap the sight:
Beethoven striding through the night!

18
AUGUST

World, what would you do without Khorazm?!

Muhammad chose this place for particular attention.
This is why Khorasm has a host of Scholars.
When the history of Khorazm is laid open,
You will see greats like Al-Khorazmiy and Beruniy.

World, what would you do without Khorazm?
You would have passed with no Al-Khorazmiy, nor Beruniy.
World, what would you do without Khorazm?
You should have passed with no Avesto, nor Zardusht.

On the day when Khorazm took the water of Jayhun-river,
Khorazm was admitted to the halls of the great.
There are its mountains of unsatisfied hopes –
Jalaliddin the brave came from this homeland.

World, what would you do without Khorazm?
You would have passed with no Jalaliddin, nor Siyavush.
World, what would you do without Khorazm?
You would have passed with no Komiljon, nor Hajihon.

Khorazm the Homeland where the master-athlete was born,
There are too the Sufis like Sultan Uvays, and Gavsil-great.
There are saints like az-Zamakhshariy, and Kubra,
There is the great singer Komiljon who praised you and,
There are scholars like Akhmad-hoji Khorazmiy.

World, what would you do without Khorazm?
You would have passed with no Agohiy, nor Mamun.
World, what would you do without Khorazm?
You would have passed with no Feruz the second, nor Akhmads.
You would have passed without the great Khorazmiys.

19
AUGUST

Мир человеческой души удивителен и таинственен. Читая книгу Марины Михайловской, словно проживаешь вместе с автором дни её жизни. Приходит понимание и осознание того, что её творчество ничто иное как путь. Путь, ведущий к храму её души. Поэтесса идёт к нему, культивируя в себе доброту и свет. Стремясь понять себя. Стремясь стать счастливее!..

— Ленифер Мамбетова, лучший женский автор
в рамках фестиваля OEBF-2014,
лаурет премии им. Марзии Закрирьяновой.

ISBN: 978-1-910886-41-0
RRP: £14.50

<table>
<tr><td>**22**</td></tr>
<tr><td>**AUGUST**</td></tr>
</table>

16 MONDAY

17 TUESDAY

18 WEDNESDAY

19 THURSDAY

20 FRIDAY

21 SATURDAY   22 SUNDAY

I want to be

I want to melt away in the deluge of your mind.
I want this flame to be for just us two to find.
I want to be an angel, and lead you by the hand to paradise,
Giving away what's not been said, and pay the sorrow's price.

I want to be a knight and guard your sleep.
I want to be the wind, so that this flame burns deep.
I want to be a shaman, and heal all of your sorrow,
Touching with my soul your gray thoughts of tomorrow

I want to be a God - forgiving all your sins that be.
I want that world where there is only you and me.
I want to be the mind - creating new words to be.
I cannot quench my thirst - you're like the water of the sea.

23
AUGUST

Wanderers Nachtlied

Über allen Gipfeln
Ist Ruh.
In allen Wipfeln
Spührest du
Kaum einen Hauch.
Die Vöglein schweigen im Walde…
Warte nur, balde
Ruhest du auch…

Night Wanderers

On mountain tops
All is still.
Everything stops.
Not a breath will
Ruffle the lofty crests.
In the woods, birds are hushed
Wait softly, do not be rushed –
You too will find rest.

28
AUGUST

In this jewellike collection of poems from Kyrgyz poet Sagyn Berkinalieva, the poet explores her own personal destiny and her memorable insights into love, plumbing the raw feelings that cut through her heart in the course of one memorable encounter. Berkinalieva's own unique and genuine voice shines through poignantly on every page.

ISBN: 978-1913356217
RRP: £12.95

29
AUGUST

23 MONDAY

24 TUESDAY

25 WEDNESDAY

26 THURSDAY

27 FRIDAY

28 SATURDAY   29 SUNDAY

AIYA MAXUTOVA (KAZAKHSTAN)

Oh, you wise poets of the East
Remember what our ancestors say
Let me treat you to a lavish feast
And sing of the true steppe way.

The tender bosom of the steppe
Was trampled brutally by the Hordes.
My nation long bewailed of this,
Barbarians scornfully use the words:
'Cattle-breeder', and 'Kyrgyz'.

Those raids and cries and poverty…
And yurts, moving like dervishes, in rags –
Like an orphan grew that steppe elm-tree.
But you revived again, oh steppe,
Your heroes gave us sturdy backs!

In countless battles Kazakhs made a stand
For honour and freedom, and for their land!

30
AUGUST

Kyrgyzstan

My Kyrgyzstan, you're the best of worlds,
You're my homeland and I feel calm here.
You don`t need a lot of colourful words,
You just want me to live truthfully and clear.
There is an eye – my precious Issyk-Kul,
Looking far into the deep of Heaven
Where snowflakes hide like lacy tulle
Under cloud waves that have always striven
To move… My Issyk-Kul, such lovely place
It won't freeze in winter, in a snowstorm
And wherever I am, I want to go home,
To where Tien Shan is draped like a necklace
Where Ala-Too is stands erect and dumb
Yet is yelling us through the centuries
About its eternal, proud right to drum:
"Value the homeland, value the memories!
Because your ancestors shed their blood
For a handful of earth, for the fatherland
They fought bravely; we dedicate a ballade
To their future families!"
We have the flag, the coat of arms today,
We sing an anthem and we have a tundyke –
This yurt roof means never betray
And stay connected with the Sun, with Nature.
Oh, tell me Issyk-Kul on a winter day
How could I not be love in you, my rapture?
Aigul will blossom in Batken in spring
The flower of the moon, it is endemic.
In Kyrgyzstan I feel like have wings
Then I`ll tell about the flower`s legend!

31
AUGUST

FALLING ASH

The old dzighit smoked by the balcony rail
As the sun softly bled in the west,
And young Aizhan flicked out her fingernail
To shake off the ash from his chest.

"Ah remember the terrible thirties when
We starved from Lysenko's plan.
Yes, so many Kazakhs died back then..."
"You told me, granddad," she began.

"Remember the monster Beria, who
Expelled us from our homes. Oh we died –
Ah so many Kazakhs died, then too..."
"We learned it at school," she replied.

"Remember the nuclear test days when
Hell on Earth it seemed had dawned.
Many Kazakhs died or fell sick then..."
"Yes, yes, this is old," she yawned.

"Then remember how our old way of life
Helped us endure and never bend.
So we Kazakhs survived this strife..."
She thumbed her phone. "It's my friend."

At that he sagged, "What a tragedy!
That we've been reduced to just this?"
But Aizhan laughed so naturally,
And gave him a quick little kiss.

"It's your triumph, granddad, not your tragedy.
"It is," she said, "Your greatest gain –
That we young can grow up so light and free,
Unburdened by your yoke of pain.

Like tulips that bloom from dirty earth.
Like the apple blossoming in spring.
So brief, so utterly frivolous from birth –
But it's the future's promise we bring."

A tear welled in the old man's eye.
He longed for her to understand.
To feel the woe that made him sigh.
But she turned and waved her hand.

"Where now?" he moaned, "The cinema –
A fantasy in an ancient land.
A warrior girl with a weird guitar.
It's cool. You won't understand..."

30 MONDAY

31 TUESDAY

01 WEDNESDAY

02 THURSDAY

03 FRIDAY

04 SATURDAY   05 SUNDAY

GENNADY FEDOROVICH SHPALIKOV (RUSSIA)

Fortunately or maybe not…

Fortunately or maybe not,
The truth is this is so:
You can never return to the same spot
That you departed long ago.

The ashes might look just as before
And smell quite similar too,
But we won't find what we're looking for
Neither me nor you.

I'd ban everyone, you know,
From journeys to the past,
And I ask as a brother: do not go –
Don't make my agony last.

Otherwise I'll take the trail –
Who'll bring back my life?
In my felt boots I would sail
To nineteen forty-five.

And when I arrive back at that year,
The year of forty-five –
My mother looks so young, so dear,
And my dad is still alive.

*The verse is recommended
by Nadin W. Weklich*

Age of Love

The time of Love, Creation and Confession,
The period of Beauty and Infinity.
The time of Glory, Values of the Nation,
The time of Gratitude and Love reality.

The time of Wealth delight
Willing of the eternal Inspiration
When people can have a Passion flight
The time of the Peace, the Art and the deep Sensation
When the Sunset turns into Sunlight

***

The time of Love, Creation and Confession
The period of Beauty and Infinity.
The time of Glory, Values of the Nation,
The time of Gratitude and Love Reality

07
SEPTEMBER

ALTYNAI TEMIROVA (KYRGYZSTAN)

All night you hear the komuz hum.
The artist is tireless, though his tongue is numb.
Sweet sounds flow out, as his soul sings
And his deft hands flicker over the strings.
Family and friends listen on in awe,
As the magic unfurls from his melodic store.
The master engages with life and death,
Forgetting all – his heart torn by every breath –
And gripping the hearts of all those around.
He sings of the present and the days to come.
And death slowly fades in the komuz's hum.
A muse of inspiration hovers in each sound.
Life slows through the night as the komuz rings.
His tongue is numb, but his soul sings.

09

SEPTEMBER

I WILL WRAP MYSELF UP IN A BLANKET

I will wrap myself up in a blanket,
And let its softness slowly calm me,
I'm telling myself not to hurry
And letting my eyes close quietly.

It's really not very often
That I can lie and let everything be –
When I'm not the centre of action,
And no-one's waiting for me.

Today, I hope they'll forget me
And manage it all without aid.
And that my ever-present shadow
Will put none of them in the shade.

I am pushing away all my worries.
They'll do fine without me there.
I'll relax here under my blanket,
And just forget every care.

12

SEPTEMBER

The hands of our ancestors are ever active. Weaving, as they do, their signs and marks into everything manifest. Hardly a surprise, on reflection, since the departed have always heavily outnumbered those presently surrounding us. Yet, realizing the unending power of our forebears may shock unwary observers, while openly unsettling the faint of heart. After all, ancestral influences can take challengingly repellent, unrepentantly grotesque, or even divinely aesthetic expression. All meaning, on the level of the Global Text, poets usually fall into a necessary burlesque when such spectres appear in verse. In which case, introducing *My Homeland, Oh My Crimea* in its first English edition is not simply an honour, but also a reminder of our common humanity. Moreover, as the first Crimean-Tartar poetry collection ever published in the English-speaking world, it is an extremely rare privilege. Certainly, Lennifer's terse and highly evocative style will delight her new readerships. Reminding them through politicized image and lamenting symbol that writer's "learn" prose, although they "express" poetry. The latter being an act of healing, along with the possibility of genuine transcendence.

ISBN: 978-1-910886-04-5
RRP: £17.50

09
SEPTEMBER

06 MONDAY

07 TUESDAY

08 WEDNESDAY

09 THURSDAY

10 FRIDAY

11 SATURDAY   12 SUNDAY

NATALIE BISSO (GERMANY)

In Autumn Streams

Oh September, don't fly away, please!
Don't call up the blizzards and their wild dance.
That your mild evenings of beautiful weather
Brings love to our hearts is not chance.

In the warm autumn, I'm not scared of the rain –
It sounds like a waltz softly pattering down.
And every tree is awaiting October
In autumn hush with its golden crown.

This soft loveliness opens our souls
And bears our dreams on leaves of gold.
Autumn streams down with fruitful change
To October shores and the coming cold.

Жакшы иштер тууралуу

Жаштык өтөт, өмүр бүтөт элирген,
Бу дүйнө — түш, сен да өтөсүң өмүрдөн.
Өмүрүңдү Ата Журтка арнасаң,
Жыргап-куунап кор болбойсуң эч качан.

Эстүүлөрдүн айткандарын билгин сен, "
Эч ким качып кутула албайт өлүмдөн"
Бул дүйнөгө далай эрлер келишкен,
 Жашап, өнүп, кез келгенде өлүшкөн.

Бек болсоң да, кул болсоң да бүт баары,
Өлөт бир күн, артта калат аттары,
Эми келди сенин дагы кезегиң,
Моюн сунуп, жакшы ишиңди өтөгүн.

17
SEPTEMBER

ABOUT GOOD DEEDS

Your youth will pass and life will pass,
This world's a dream, and dies like grass.
If you give your life up to our land,
Head held high you'll always stand.

The knowledge that all wise men have:
"No one escapes the sting of death".
So many men have lived on this earth,
They grew and died and gave new birth.

All are the same: the rich, the poor –
With time their names will be no more.
What any person really needs
Is to be good and do good deeds.

18
SEPTEMBER

13 MONDAY

14 TUESDAY

15 WEDNESDAY

16 THURSDAY

17 FRIDAY

18 SATURDAY   19 SUNDAY

TATIANA KULIKOVA (KALMYKIA, RUSSIA)

Golden Autumn

Once more, golden autumn knocks at my window,
And my thoughts whirl like dry leaves on the breeze,
I'd like to break the rules and go back long ago
When we first walked among autumn trees.

Back to a time when our thoughts and our feelings
Were so childish, so innocent, and so true,
When we both confessed, our love revealing...
Do you remember? It was just me and you.

Do you remember the night we came together?
We walked through the moonlight and walked very far.
And do you remember our shared reverie?
And how at last we kissed under a star?

Do you remember whispering love's sweet words,
Witnessed only by the falling leaves.
There was no-one around, just the birds –
The whole wide world was for us, we believed.

Alas, we cannot turn back time at all,
But I so wish be there, please
On the moonlit night of our first leaf fall,
And our first walk among autumn trees.

20

SEPTEMBER

The most precious person
*(Dedicated to the most precious person of my life,
my husband Alexander Kulikov)*

You are a gift from up above,
I wouldn't live without you near;
You are my refuge, my true love,
My precious man, my very dear.

Your breath, your voice and your kiss –
So sweet to me, my heart, my own!
The love in your eyes I cannot miss.
You know I live for you alone.

I love your hands, their soft caress.
I love your handsome face.
And I'm impatient, I confess,
To be held in your embrace.

If you're gone just a minute or two,
The ache's too much to bear,
I live with you, I live for you –
I'm breathing with your air.

ALEKSANDRA VLASOVA (UK)

***

The rainy autumn blues,
The leaves that dance through chilling gusts.
A union of hearts suffuse,
On tables, fashion magazines are thrust.

Hot coffee sits in pretty mugs,
And steaming cups of honey flavoured tea.
This for me, this is how our Autumn snugs,
Wrapped up all cosy – that's how it should be.

Autumn Sorrow

I welcome you, my autumn sorrow.
It feels like there is no tomorrow.
An empty space inside my soul
Is dark and nothing will console.

I crave for summer's light and glow,
When clouds passed slowly to and fro.
The thoughts were drowsy in my mind...
This happy time is left behind.

The night will bring me Stygian gloom
And deepen silence in my room.
Aroint thee, my autumn sorrow!
I'm looking forward to tomorrow!

24
SEPTEMBER

To Autumn

Season of mists and mellow fruitfulness,
   Close bosom-friend of the maturing sun;
Conspiring with him how to load and bless
   With fruit the vines that round the thatch-eves run;
To bend with apples the moss'd cottage-trees,
   And fill all fruit with ripeness to the core;
     To swell the gourd, and plump the hazel shells
   With a sweet kernel; to set budding more,
And still more, later flowers for the bees,
Until they think warm days will never cease,
     For Summer has o'er-brimm'd their clammy cells.

Who hath not seen thee oft amid thy store?
   Sometimes whoever seeks abroad may find
Thee sitting careless on a granary floor,
   Thy hair soft-lifted by the winnowing wind;
Or on a half-reap'd furrow sound asleep,
   Drows'd with the fume of poppies, while thy hook
     Spares the next swath and all its twined flowers:
And sometimes like a gleaner thou dost keep
   Steady thy laden head across a brook;
   Or by a cyder-press, with patient look,
     Thou watchest the last oozings hours by hours.

Where are the songs of Spring? Ay, where are they?
   Think not of them, thou hast thy music too —
While barred clouds bloom the soft-dying day,
   And touch the stubble-plains with rosy hue;
Then in a wailful choir the small gnats mourn
   Among the river sallows, borne aloft
     Or sinking as the light wind lives or dies;
And full-grown lambs loud bleat from hilly bourn;
   Hedge-crickets sing; and now with treble soft
   The red-breast whistles from a garden-croft;
     And gathering swallows twitter in the skies

26

SEPTEMBER

20 MONDAY

21 TUESDAY

22 WEDNESDAY

23 THURSDAY

24 FRIDAY

25 SATURDAY

26 SUNDAY

Autumn

In the autumn... when the soil is dead –
When the soils are pale in the falling time.
For the last time, when the leaf turns red –
When the leaves are red for the last time.

Crows croak in empty gardens but
Whose fate are they bewailing?
They fiercely clutch the fallen nut.
Yet whose final hope is failing?

You ice-clad folk from lands that freeze:
Leave your foul dreams there in the snow.
You stole the fruit from my orchard trees:
May your black heads be buried below!

Who knows whose hopes have now been lost
In the falling time when the leaves turn red?
Whose destiny's withered with the frost
In the autumn...when the soil is dead.

29

SEPTEMBER

I believe in a people's generation

Will anyone grieve when a poet dies?
Would they say kind and thoughtful things?
When the apple blossom withers and dries,
Is there the sad comfort a new sonnet brings?
Let the echoes of my lines not shake
The memories of years passed away.
Let this new time become awake
With the living, the people of today.
Yes, I believe in a people's generation.
I believe in myself in every way,
In the blue cranes flying on migration,
Carefully holding my fate in play.

We live our lives the best we can?

What can I do to stop my youth fading away?
To keep my beauty always fresh as the day
For my skin to stay silky, and my body move swiftly.
For life to be fun, and never lived passively.
But youth slips away, without any heed.
Old age barges in and locks on its prey.
If old age hesitated a moment indeed
Everyone would be grateful for the delay.
Well, we content ourselves with what must be,
Live the best we can, and regret seeing
The years fly by, that life leaves in a hurry,
But brings a new generation into being.

01
OCTOBER

SOORONBAI JUSUEV (KYRGYZSTAN)

Short extract from 'Kurmanjan-Datka'

1.
The dazzling brilliance of the skies
Soars over the heights of Ala-Too.
And the vivid green carpet lies
Like a paradise laid out for you.

2.
And the Kyrgyz of these mountains are
Like a bow bent back with arrow ready.
The old ways shine on like a star
Burning tireless on and steady!

3.
Glistening glaciers with mirror gleams,
Melting to gush out over boulders,
And the quenching freshness of their streams
Bubbles down the mountains' shoulders.

5.
Eagles swoop over this mountain land.
With nightingales' song, the woods are bent.
Like the gentle caress of a young girl's hand,
Your memory dissolves in nature's scent.

6.
Take pleasure in the warming sun,
And the deep beauty of nature's creation.
Here our lion-hearted hero Manas was one
With the free spirit of the Kyrgyz nation!

7.
Here gold and precious gemstones lie –
Our people's wealth and treasure chest.
But from England, Russia, China spies
Entered this land to rob and wrest,
Travelling the Silk Road from east and west.

8.
Many took the Great Silk Road,
And their caravans found welcome here.
But whenever enemies evil showed,
We'd die to save our land so dear.

9.
We were willing to lay down our lives.
Yes, we slayed our foes upon the field!
Despite attacks, our land survives –
If we stay together, we need not yield.

10.
In defence of our land we never tire;
Our blood is given to this nation!
And we recall our ancestors' bravery's fire,
Saving land and honour from humiliation.

11.
With lion-hearted Manas at their head,
They were generous and full of care,
And the ladies wise, honorable and steady –
Among them Kurkmanjan, queen most rare.

03

OCTOBER

27 MONDAY

28 TUESDAY

29 WEDNESDAY

30 THURSDAY

01 FRIDAY

02 SATURDAY   03 SUNDAY

CLEVELAND'S SONG

Farewell! Farewell! the voice you hear,
Has left its last soft tone with you,-
Its next must join the seaward cheer,
And shout among the shouting crew.

The accents which I scarce could form
Beneath your frown's controlling check,
Must give the word, above the storm,
To cut the mast, and clear the wreck.

The timid eye I dared not raise,-
The hand, that shook when press'd to thine,
Must point the guns upon the chase-
Must bid the deadly cutlass shine.

To all I love, or hope, or fear,-
Honour, or own, a long adieu!
To all that life has soft and dear,
Farewell! save memory of you!

04

OCTOBER

Кӧгчіл ыры (KHAKASSIAN)

Анымчох! Анымчох! - Ӱнім хулааӊа
Сарналча час табыснаӊ сағаа, нымзаанаӊ...
Паза соӊ кӧглерім талайлар салғаанда
Тар-сағыл ухтар чіли суулир тар чаанаӊ!

Чазых сӧстерімніӊ сындыр хуйағын
Китирзіӊ кӧстеріӊніӊ хырии пулиинча:
Сӧзіӊ сыйлап син чайхирзыӊ талайыӊ,
Кимемні сындырып, толғап иӊ тириинче.

Тын пазынып, час кӧрізім чочынып,
Сірлеен салааларнаӊ синзерӧк тартылча -
Мылтых атхан чіли кӧглерімнеӊ тартызып,
Хылыс хал чанынаӊ сыр ханым урылча...

Пу чир парчазына - хыныс, ізеніс, соохха,
Чӱрексіс чарығы сын Ээлерге, чонға,
Чуртас сілии салғағы-талай оохха,
Йа, Анымчох! Сын кӧӧм пар - улусха!

Translation
by Tom Sibday

05

OCTOBER

YULIA OLSHEVSKAYA-HATZENBOLLER (RUSSIA)

Babylonian heights of an emerald green night…

Babylonian heights
in an emerald green night,
And the blinding white glow
of lace on a new wedding dress…
All the slings of swirling words intertwined
- strong and bright
In Rodin's antique pattern -
in Spring's unbreakable embrace…

A brief flash woven honey –
of Ladenburg silver lace,
Of multi-faceted parks,
weighed down with fresh Christmas snow…
And my Orient Express
continuing the eternal race
In the flickering blank
of an age of blizzard's icy blow…

And those roses so lone,
strewn around by a lady's thin hand,
Placed in a tight window frame tight –
like a bright fan on parquet!..
But with Modigliani's fine stroke -
both lively and voiceless still life stand –
One'll repeat, an unknown -
with the morning flamboyant bouquet -
The name of the Rose.

06

OCTOBER

04 MONDAY

05 TUESDAY

06 WEDNESDAY

07 THURSDAY

08 FRIDAY

09 SATURDAY   10 SUNDAY

Amor, che nel penser mio vive et regna

Love, that lives in and governs my thought
And makes in my heart his chief throneplace,
Sometimes, fully armed, takes over my face
And encamps, flying the mark of his court.
Yet she, who taught me to love and feel pain,
Now wants to suffocate my ardour's flame
With reason and a reverent shame,
And is vexed by our passion once again!

And so timid Love flees to my heart
To collapse there, weeping and shaken;
He bows his frail head and trembles apart.
Oh, what can I do but take my lord's part
And stand by him until he is taken.
There's no better end: to love well and depart.

Pace non trovo, e non ho da far Guerra

There is no peace for me, yet I cannot make war;
I fear, but I hope; I burn, yet I'm cold;
I soar to the skies, and plunge to Earth's floor;
I'm clutching at nothing, then embrace the world
whole.
I'm trapped in a prison, with no bars nor way
loose;
My jailor can't keep me, nor unbind my ties,
And Love will not hang me, nor let go my noose;
It bars me from living, yet won't let me die.

I see without eyes; I cry with no voice;
I long so to perish, yet pray for some aid;
I hate myself keenly, yet love someone too;
I'm nourished by sadness, weeping rejoice;
Of both death and life, I'm just as afraid.
To this state I've succumbed, my lady, for you.

12
OCTOBER

València. Infanta made of granite.

for my son, Michael

Why break in? The door is open.
A flame is smouldering on the hearth.
I'm a granite stone Infanta,
Passing ages miles apart.

Dots are melting into space,
Whirling endlessly away.
Oh, this little baby face,
Dear son in warm embrace,
You were born on this same day.

Can you take a soul from stones?
At the time of long Farewell
I'm in a labyrinth of high walls
Of occurrences' strange spell.

Can things happen with cast lots?
Is that a white flag up there –
Curtains with those polka dots?
As a sprout, grown in a pot,
Yesterday again would spire.

Cautiously I walk down here,
A white day – it melts and whirls,
All that was so hard, not near,
Now all sprouts and quickly grows...

14
OCTOBER

DANA ZHETEYEVA (KAZAKHSTAN)

Kokshetau (excerpt)

Kokshetau mount is as gracile as pines,
It washes its face with the waters of rain.
And clouds that float just above its crown,
Inquire after its health and well-being.

It's surrounded densely by eighty pure lakes,
Each of them lies in a golden lavabo.
Come here, my friend, if you are in pain,
The air of steppe will help you recover.

Tall pine-trees always grow on that mound,
And birch-trees are covered in sheltering green.
The wind will frolic on the grass and florets,
And brush them in the rays of early mornings.

The pines grow at the very peak too,
Their roots are so strong, they'll never let go of
The tree trunks. And the mount is lofty as well,
Only hawks can make their nests right up there.

The peak is all mantled with mauve and dense fog,
And none of the arrows ever reached its top.
If only a soul could inhale that clean air,
One wouldn't forget it until he's in heaven.

The moment the sun is kissing the peak,
The hills around turn golden in a blink.
The bottomless pit of all times is revealed then,
The ages will pass by you then in procession.

15

OCTOBER

11 MONDAY

12 TUESDAY

13 WEDNESDAY

14 THURSDAY

15 FRIDAY

16 SATURDAY

17 SUNDAY

English and Russian translations of
Tala'a-l-Badru 'alayna (طلع البدر علينا) –
Таля'а-ль-бадру аляйна

Tala'a-l-Badru 'alaynā
Min thaniyyāti-l-Wadā',
Wajaba-sh-shukru 'alaynā,
Mā da'ā lillāhi dā'.

Ayyuha-l-mab'ūthu fīnā,
Ji'ta bil-amri-l-mutā',
Ji'ta sharrafta-l-Madīnah,
Marhaban, yā khayra dā'.

Oh, the full moon rose over us
From the Valley of Wadā',
And we ought to show gratefulness,
While there is a call to Allah.

Our Messenger, you're amongst us
with the real life from our God,
You have brought to this town nobleness,
Welcome! Oh, the Caller to Success.

Полная луна взошла для нас
Над долиною Уадаа.
Мы должны быть благодарны,
Ведь к Аллаху зовут нас!

О, Пророк наш, ты среди нас
С наставленьем праведным!
Ты покрыл Медину славою,
Ждём тебя, Божий Призыв!

18

OCTOBER

طَلَعَ الْبَدْرُ عَلَيْنَا
مِنْ ثَنِيَّاتِ الْوَدَاع
وَجَبَ الْشُكْرُ عَلَيْنَا
مَا دَعَا لِلهِ دَاع

أَيُّهَا الْمَبْعُوثُ فِينَا
جِئْتَ بِالْأَمْرِ الْمُطَاع
جِئْتَ شَرَّفْتَ الْمَدِينَة
مَرْحَبًا يَا خَيْرَ دَاع

Kazakh translation of Tala'a-l-Badru 'alayna (طلع البدر علينا) – Казахский перевод – Қазақша аудармасы

Талə'ə-л-бəдру 'əлəйнə,
мин төниййəти-л-ўəдə'
ўəжəбə-ш-шукру 'əлəйнə,
мə дə'ə лиллəһи дə'.

Әййуһə-л-мəб'уθу фийнə
жи'тə би-л-əмри-л-мута'
Жи'та шəррафтə-л-Мəдийнəһ
Мархəбəн йə хайра дə'

Шықты біз үшін толған ай
Уада деген аңғарынан
Тиіспіз риза болуға
Иманға шақырылғанда

Аллаһ арамыздан таңдаған,
Оны тыңдауға шақырған,
Мединені ұлықтаған,
Қош келдің, Мейірімді Ұран!

19
OCTOBER

Translation of Marina Tsvetayeva

* * *

There's one made of stone, and the other – of clay,
But I'm all silver and glee.
My name's Marina, my whim's to betray.
A mortal sea foam – that's me.

For some made of clay, for some made of flesh
The end is a tombstone and grave –
Baptized in the sea, I'll be, certainly, smashed
In my sparkling flight on the wave.

But I will break through every heart, every chain.
You cannot but see my loose curls
And know that any attempt is in vain –
I won't be the salt of the earth.

With every new billow I'll be reborn
First, splintered on your granite knees.
Long live the bright foam whose life goes on,
The jolly, high foam of the seas!

Translated by Irene Yavchunovsky

20
OCTOBER

Ancestors

A divinely 'stolen' bride,
a love forever divine,
dwelling in divine happiness…
Guarding your threshold
lay a white Snow Leopard from the white mountains,
smelling of glaciers,
always ready to jump, fierce.

The son of Umai[1] and Tengri[2] in Heaven was he,
stately and beautifully built,
and, as the Most High, possessing everything,
generously bestowed on him by Heaven.
The sun shone in the sky,
always accompanying his deeds.

And keeping that sacred covenant,
He tirelessly strove into the sky…
From sunrise to sunset,
from East to West…
is this turning of the cycle of Fate?

The Milky Way spilled by him
scattered seeds of immortality…
Heavenly clouds poured into
the bowl with his white foam koumiss[3].
From this overflowing keker[4]
splashed life-giving moisture
and seeped into the bosom of the earth.
Do not exhaust us for many centuries,
and do not unravel us like a wonderful dream!

1 Umai is the goddess of the hearth and family

2 Tengri is the god of heaven

3 Koumiss is a national drink made from mare's milk

4 A keker is a vessel made of leather for drinking koumiss.

23
OCTOBER

To Mark

The birds made of steel long for the sky
Forgotten passports gather dust way up high
You begin to lost track of both dawn and the dusk
Those times at plane windows were ever so brusk

You liked the spots by the window or by the aisle with snacks
You like to believe that the sorrow you hold has passed its climax
It's probably time to stop, take a break?
To start again stronger for your own very sake

On the road in the sky to your dreams, to your loved ones
We will sit in steel birds, guarded by luck of the high ones
So that you can see new disks and new dawns
And new people's hello and goodbyes you will treat as if bronze

24

OCTOBER

18 MONDAY

19 TUESDAY

20 WEDNESDAY

21 THURSDAY

22 FRIDAY

23 SATURDAY   24 SUNDAY

COUNTY GUY

Ah! County Guy, the hour is nigh,
The sun has left the lea,
The orange flower perfumes the bower,
The breeze is on the sea.
The lark his lay who thrill'd all day
Sits hush'd his partner nigh:
Breeze, bird, and flower confess the hour,
But where is County Guy?

The village maid steals through the shade,
Her shepherd's suit to hear;
To beauty shy, by lattice high,
Sings high-born Cavalier.
The star of Love, all stars above
Now reigns o'er earth and sky;
And high and low the influence know-
But where is County Guy?

25

OCTOBER

Φίλε μου, που είσαι. (GREEK)

Η ώρα ήρθε, φίλε μου,
Ο ήλιος έχει δύσει,
Μεθά το άρωμα τ' ανθού,
Δροσιά έχει φυσήσει.
Πετά το άσμα του πουλιού
Και έχει σταματήσει:
Ειν' όλα για την χάρη σου.
Μα, φίλε μου, που είσαι;

Μια κόρη ψάχνει τον βοσκό
Κρυφά ν'αγκαλιαστούν,
Και άλλοι την πανσέληνο
Μαζί να μοιραστούν.
Ο έρωτας είναι το παν,
Σαν τ'άστρα θα γυαλίσει,
Καθένας κάποιον αγαπα -
Μα, φίλε μου, που είσαι;

Translation by Alina Moseykina

26

OCTOBER

This collection of poetry is the first book in Azerbaijani written by the talented young poet Leyla Aliyeva, who is known in our iterary circles for moving poems, such as *"Don't Go, Mother"*, *"I will Go and Cry a Little"*, *"The Swan"*, *"The Butterfly"*, *"To Each Their Own End"* and "I am Blind". From her very first work, these poems have shown her own way of thinking and distinctive view of the world. They are like unfading flowers that retain sorrow, love, the warmth of the air, rain, drizzle and scent. For several years now Leyla Aliyeva has been earning the admiration of a wide, intellectual readership.

ISBN: 978-1-910886-76-2
RRP: £19.50

31
OCTOBER

25 MONDAY

26 TUESDAY

27 WEDNESDAY

28 THURSDAY

29 FRIDAY

30 SATURDAY

31 SUNDAY

I Let out birds

The day is done – all its affairs and words
And petty cares are past. My soul's at rest.
And now, with dawn's first rays, I'll let out birds,
Birds born of inspiration, from my breast.

You, in the name of honour waging battle,
To you flies my first gift through the heavens' blue.
There, high above the clouds in sunshine bathing
A mighty eagle spreads its wings for you.

You, travellers, though weary, full of cheer,
To you I send a crane at chilly dawn.
A cuckoo that will promise you long years
I send you who are ailing and forlorn.

You lovers! For your sake a nightingale
I send to sing, impassioned, all night long.
You separated souls! A snow-white dove
Bring you new hope to make your spirits strong.

You who are in despair; you timid-souled,
To every one of you my birds set out.
Yet naught have I for those whose hearts are cold.
No birds for them-they'll have to do without.

The day is done – all its affairs and words
And petty cares are past. My soul's at rest.
And now, with dawn's first rays, l'll let out birds,
Birds born of inspiration, from my breast.

Translated by Dorian Rottenberg

01
NOVEMBER

My Home

My home is always there,in the heaven's vault,
    Where one just hears lyre's sounds,
All with a spark of life have here their resort,
    A bard has, too, a space around.
It gets the farthest stars by edges of his roof,
    And from a wall to one another
There is a path whose measure can be proved
    Not by a look, but by a soul, rather.
A sense of basic truth in every soul nests —
    The seed that's sacred and eternal:
In flesh of time it always can embrace
    Space, endless, and the century's kernel.

And mighty God has built for this exclusive sense
    My home of the light and wonders,
And only here I'm doomed to sufferings at length,
    And only here — to calmness.

Мой дом

Мой дом везде, где есть небесный свод,
    Где только слышны звуки песен.
Всё, в чем есть искра жизни, в нём живет,
    Но для поэта он не тесен.
До самых звезд он кровлей досягает,
    И от одной стены к другой —
Далекий путь, который измеряет
    Жилец не взором, но душой.
Есть чувство правды в сердце человека,
    Святое вечности зерно:
Пространство без границ, теченье века
    Объемлет в краткий миг оно.
И всемогущим мой прекрасный дом
    Для чувства этого построен,
И осужден страдать я долго в нём,
    И в нём лишь буду я спокоен.

05

NOVEMBER

***

Здесь Лола, всем родня,
Сияет в блеске дня,
И с ней подруга Атиргул –
Сто языков огня.

Несчетно у реки
Толпяться васильки.
И дружит с красным синий цвет,
Как в песне две строки.

Там, где цветут цветы,
Сбываются мечты,
И сказка переходит в явь
Там, где цветут цветы.

Но по округе всей
Сильнее нет страстей,
Чем вера и любовь Наргис.
Как быть, что делать ей?

И птица, и цветок,
И горный ручеек,
Мы песней в честь ее любви
Приблизим счастья срок.

Пускай в урочный час
Бамбур услышит нас,
Чтоб отразиться у Рагис
В глубинах черных глаз.

***

Here Lola, friend to all,
Shines in the glorious day.
Companion Atirgul beside her –
A hundred tongues of flame.

Countless by the river
Cornflowers crowd and cluster.
The red makes friends with blue
Like two lines of a song.

There, where flowers grow
Even dreams can come to life.
The world reveals its fairy tales
There, where flowers grow

Yet nowhere in that land can be
A passion stronger than this:
The certainty of Nargis' love.
How does she live, what can she do?

And the flowers and the birds
And the tumbling mountain streams
With song in honour of her love
Will hasten her time of joy.

So let it be, at the appointed hour
Bambur will hear our song,
That his reflection once again
May fall on Nargis' deep black eyes

07

NOVEMBER

01 MONDAY

02 TUESDAY

03 WEDNESDAY

04 THURSDAY

05 FRIDAY

06 SATURDAY

07 SUNDAY

I'm not ashamed…

The sun has burned its circle out,
Leaving the stars to parade in the sky
And you came by, fooling all no doubt.
My beloved, my dear, you came by.

I will press myself against your chest
In spite of the watching crowd,
Although my conscience says it's not for the best.
"I'm not ashamed," I whisper aloud.

I'm not ashamed. I'll steal just one night
For the lonely longing I've known.
I will hug you. I will hold you tight.
I'll enchant you with my love alone.

"Mine. Only mine!" I intone like a spell
Grateful for my fate bittersweet.
For a happy moment I'm riding the carousel –
"I'm not ashamed," I repeat.

Not ashamed. But lonely, and in love.
I'm just clinging on to some hope.
I've snatched a scrap from the feast above –
I'm human and it's how I cope.

Not ashamed. But my heart is weeping,
Poisoning our minutes of bliss.
All through the night there's bitterness seeping
Into every honeyed kiss.

I will never forget this time with you.
From your touch, my body still moans,
I'm not ashamed. But I want to howl too.
And I will cry on my bed quite alone.

<table>
<tr><td>

08

NOVEMBER

</td></tr>
</table>

Rock

A lonely rock stands by a lonely path
It has stood here for over a thousand years
From when gods were born and brought their wrath
To current days when they had disappeared

It is a witness to countless generations
And can retell every fairy tale told
Perhaps our ancestors bend knees to it in aspiration
And worshipped it as a god to behold

But that old form had been eroded
For time had scratched at its display
All that's left is stone that's been corroded
A symbol of silence, death and decay

And now, these days, when gods have passed
Perhaps the time has come for it to speak at last

I hope that one day it will meet a creator
One with a chisel, who will use it as a canvas
And he will work through heat and rain and greater
To give life to that which came from blackness

And one day, as if from a heavy fog
It will realize all that it has dreamt to be
Not as before, some rock you find in some bog
But as a symbol of heavenly degree

And when the chisel's done and gladdened
And the master of craft wipes sweat from his head
The stone will be there tell all that has happened
And will continue to do so in the artist's stead

12
NOVEMBER

Дилдора Туляганова родом из Ташкента (Узбекистан). Ее мировосприятие формировалось под влиянием творчества Алишера Навои, Бабура, Омар Хайяма, Пушкина, Есенина и других. Позже буквально заболела творчеством великих просветителей джадидского движения Центральной Азии, таких как Бехбудий, Фитрат, Мунаввар Кори Абдурашидханова. В дальнейшем это вылилось в передачу «Ёнмаган ёзувлар» (Рукописи не горят) на Узбекском Государственном ТВ. В 1999 году, пригласили работать в «Интерньюс», затем на радио «Свобода». В 2010 году, по заказу ТРТ (Турецкой телерадиовещательной корпорации) сняла 7 документальных фильмов о диаспорах живущих в Узбекистане (уйгуры, казахи, дунгане, азербайджанцы, башкиры, поляки, русские). Участник международных научных конференций. Профессиональный журналист-исследователь, сценарист, фотограф. Поэт.

ISBN: 978-1-910886-83-0
RRP: £9.50

14

NOVEMBER

08 MONDAY

09 TUESDAY

10 WEDNESDAY

11 THURSDAY

12 FRIDAY

13 SATURDAY   14 SUNDAY

IT WAS AN ENGLISH LADYE BRIGHT

It was an English ladye bright,
(The sun shines fair on Carlisle wall,)
And she would marry a Scottish knight,
For Love will still be lord of all.

Blithely they saw the rising sun
When he shone fair on Carlisle wall;
But they were sad ere day was done,
Though Love was still the lord of all.

Her sire gave brooch and jewel fine,
Where the sun shines fair on Carlisle wall;
Her brother gave but a flask of wine,
For ire that Love was lord of all.

For she had lands both meadow and lea,
Where the sun shines fair on Carlisle wall,
And he swore her death, ere he would see
A Scottish knight the lord of all.

That wine she had not tasted well
(The sun shines fair on Carlisle wall,)
When dead, in her true love's arms, she fell,
For Love was still the lord of all!

He pierced her brother to the heart,
Where the sun shines fair on Carlisle wall:--
So perish all would true love part
That Love may still be lord of all!
And then he took the cross divine,
Where the sun shines fair on Carlisle wall,
And died for her sake in Palestine;
So Love was still the lord of all.

Now all ye lovers, that faithful prove,
(The sun shines fair on Carlisle wall,)
Pray for their souls who died for love,
For Love shall still be lord of all!

15

NOVEMBER

Эта яркая девчонка из Англии (RUSSIAN)

Эта яркая девчонка, хоть из Англии она,
(солнце светит для всех над стенáми Карлайла)
Скоро выйдет за шотландца, славного рыцаря,
Ведь Любовь будет как прежде царить над всем.

Вместе им встречать рассветы
На стенáх Карлайла;
Но загрустили ещё до заката,
Хоть Любовь как прежде царила над всем.

Её отец дал броши и каменья,
Когда солнце светило над стенами Карлайла,
Её брат дал одну лишь флягу вина,
Недовольный, что Любовь царила над всем.

Поскольку она владела землями с лугами и полями,
Там, где солнце светило над стенами Карлайла,
А он поклялся, что скорее она погибнет, чем он увидит,
Как шотландский рыцарь станет царить над всем.

Не распробовала она вино
(Когда солнце светило над стенами Карлайла),
Как уж пала мертвая на руки своего любимого,
Поскольку до тех пор Любовь царила над всем!

Он проткнул сердце её брата,
Там, где солнце светило над стенáми Карлайла:--
Так погибнут все, если возлюбленные разлучáтся,
Чтобы Любовь могла как прежде царить над всем!
И взял тогда он крест святой
Там, где солнце светило над стенáми Карлайла,
И погиб в Палестине с её именем на устах,
Так что Любовь, как прежде, царила над всем.

Так все вы, возлюбленные, докажите свою
верность,
Там, где солнце светит над стенáми Карлайла:
Почтите молитвой тех, кто пал за любовь,
Что Любовь как прежде царила над всем!

Translated by Tatiana Vasilieva

16

NOVEMBER

ქარი ქრის, ქარი ქრის, ქარი ქრის
ფოთლები მიჰქრიან ქარდაქარ
ხეთა რიგს, ხეთა ჯარს რკალად ხრის
სადა ხარ, სადა ხარ, სადა ხარ.
ისევ წვიმს, ისევ თოვს, ისევ თოვს
ვერ გპოვებ ვერასდროს, ვერასდროს
შენი მე ხატება დამდევს თან,
ყოველთვის, ყოველ დროს, ყოველგან
შორი ცა ნისლიან ფიქრებს ცრის,
ქარი ქრის, ქარი ქრის, ქარი ქრის.

THE WIND BLOWS

The wind blows, the wind blows, the wind blows…
It carries dry leaves off and away.
The tops of the trees are bending low.
Where are you? Where are you? Please say.
It rains, and it snows, and it snows…
I will never again see your face.
But the image of you brightly glows –
Always, any time. any place.
In the far distant sky, cloudy thoughts repose
And the wind blows, the wind blows, the wind blows …

17

NOVEMBER

15 MONDAY

16 TUESDAY

17 WEDNESDAY

18 THURSDAY

19 FRIDAY

20 SATURDAY

21 SUNDAY

THE DYING BARD

I. Dinas Emlinn, lament; for the moment is nigh,
When mute in the woodlands thine echoes shall die:
No more by sweet Teivi Cadwallon shall rave,
And mix his wild notes with the wild dashing wave.

II. In spring and in autumn thy glories of shade
Unhonour'd shall flourish, unhonour'd shall fade;
For soon shall be lifeless the eye and the tongue,
That view'd them with rapture, with rapture that sung.

III. Thy sons, Dinas Emlinn, may march in their pride,
And chase the proud Saxon from Prestatyn's side;
But where is the harp shall give life to their name?
And where is the bard shall give heroes their fame?

IV. And oh, Dinas Emlinn! thy daughters so fair,
Who heave the white bosom, and wave the dark hair;
What tuneful enthusiast shall worship their eye,
When half of their charms with Cadwallon shall die?

V. Then adieu, silver Teivi! I quit thy loved scene,
To join the dim choir of the bards who have been;
With Lewarch, and Meilor, and Merlin the Old,
And sage Taliessin, high harping to hold.

VI. And Adieu, Dinas Emlinn! still green be thy shades,
Unconquer'd thy warriors, and matchless thy maids!
And thou, whose faint warblings my weakness can tell,
Farewell, my loved Harp! my last treasure, farewell!

22

NOVEMBER

Умирающий бард (RUSSIAN)

I. Динас Эмлинн, плачь, ибо близок тот миг,
Когда затихнет твоё эхо в лесах:
Больше не будет Кадвалон бесноваться у сладких вод Тейви
и вплетать своё безумный рёв в дикие стремительные волны.

II. Весною и осенью их славы оттенок,
Бесславно расцветший, бесславно увянет;
И скоро безжизненны станут и глаза, что взирали на них с восторгом, и язык, что с восторгом им пел.

III. Твои сыны, Динас Эмлинн, могут шагать величаво
И преследовать горделивых саксов со стороны Престатина ;
Но где та арфа, что воспоёт их имена?
И где тот бард, что восславит подвиги героев?

IV. О, Динас Эмлинн! Честны твои дочери,
Что вплетают белые цветы в тёмные косы;
Но где тот музыкант, что восхвалит их взоры,
Когда половина их очарования растает с падением Кадвалона?

V. Так прощай же, серебряная Тейфи! Я покидаю твои возлюбленные берега,
Чтобы присоединиться к смутному хору бардов, ушедших раньше:
к Леварху и Мейлору, и Мерлину Старцу,
и мудрецу Талиессину, высоко державшему арфу.

VI. Прощай же, Динас Эмлинн! Всё ещё зелена твоя сень,
Не побеждены твои воины и не осквернены их невесты!
И ты, чьи слабеющие напевы способны выдать мои слабости,
Прощай, моя возлюбленная Арфа! Моё последнее сокровище, прощай!

*Translated
by Tatiana Vasilieva*

23

NOVEMBER

SERGEY PROTYANOV (RUSSIA)

***

My turn will come some day,
And they will be blown away, driven to the edge...
And the sky will be black and impenetrable
To all those banished from Paradise...

Life has been a rollercoaster for me more than once
And more than once I was shot in the back...
Everyone was whispering, " So when are you going to die?"
They all waited for me to disappear...
But I was not lost in this world...

You sowed evil, you sowed good-
You were infallible as the truth...
Adam's rib is curved…

<table>
<tr><td>

25

NOVEMBER

</td></tr>
</table>

22 MONDAY

23 TUESDAY

24 WEDNESDAY

25 THURSDAY

26 FRIDAY

27 SATURDAY   28 SUNDAY

***

Now come, dear friend, and listen to me -
Don't be troubled by the world; just let it be.
Let patience be your cornerstone.
Watch the world go by, and just be free.

I'm not afraid to leave life here.
I may live on for many a year.
But when it's time for me go,
I will face my fate without any fear.

Listen, it's the eternal deal, be sure:
The poor man's enemy is the poor.
These two will fight and in the middle
This world will end. That's the score.

30

NOVEMBER

Сўзимга қулоқ ос, эй дўсти аъло,
Дунё ишларини ўйлама асло.
Қаноат гўшасин айлабон макон
Олам ишларини қилғил тамошо

Кетишдан қўрқмайман мен бу дунёда,
Чунки у дунёда умрим зиёда,
Вақти етгач танда омонат жонни
Топширайин шундай бўлгач ирода.

Тингланг бу абадий савдо бўёқ лаби,
Гадонинг душмани гадо бўлади,
 Иккиси бир-бири боргунча то,
Ўртада бу дунё адо бўлади.

Translated to Kyrzys
by Sagyn Berkinalieva

04

DECEMBER

KEMEROVO: IN REQUIEM

In Grenfell, Parkland, Kemerovo
The children cry in terror.
The heads of state respond as one
What an unforeseeable error!

Last desperate calls from mobiles:
"I love you, dad. Goodbye!"
The heads of state respond as one
It's so sad they came to die.

The terror mounts, the children sob;
There's no way out of here!
The heads of state respond as one
There is no need for fear.

The bullets spray, the fire roars,
Then suddenly all is quiet,
The heads of state respond as one
Our fault? We deny it.

A man breaks down; he's lost his wife,
Three children and their aunt.
The heads of state respond as one
Can we help you? No we can't.

The authorities promise in time
An official investigation.
The heads of state, when asked how long
Say: There must be full deliberation.

But when a foreign spy is poisoned,
The truth is found in hours.
The heads of state know just what to do:
We must unite our powers!

Millions of children raise their voices
Across the USA,
And the heads of state respond at once
Expel diplomats today!

Donald, Theresa, Vladimir:
May you never sleep at night!
Or may your dreams be filled with screams
Of children lost in fright.

I weep for you, you innocents:
Boys and girls I never knew.
I weep for you their loved ones,
Whose lives were ripped in two.

05

DECEMBER

29 MONDAY

30 TUESDAY

01 WEDNESDAY

02 THURSDAY

03 FRIDAY

04 SATURDAY

05 SUNDAY

MAXIM ADAMOVICH BOGDANOVICH (BELARUS)

Pahonia

Whensoever my anxious heart, trembling With fear for our land, starts to bleed, The
Vostraja Gate I remember,
And the warriors on their dread steeds.

Flecked with white foam, those steeds, onward straining, Gallop and charge, grimly snort...
Pahonia of Old Lithuania,
None can conquer them, stay them or halt.

Into measureless distances flying, Behind you, before, years extend... After whom do ye
chase, swiftly hieing,
Where lie your paths, whither they wend?

Maybe, Belarus, they are racing After thy sons, neglectful of thee,
Who forgot thee, thy memory effacing,
Sold, betrayed thee into slavery.

Strike them deep in the heart with swords brandished!
Let them not into foreigners turn!
Let them feel in the night their hearts' anguish For their true native land ache and burn...

My dear Mother, my own Mother-Country,
Let there never be end to that ache...
Forgive! Take back thy son in thy bounty, Permit him to die for thy sake!

The steeds fly and fly, onward straining, Silver harness resounds in assault,
Pahonia of Old Lithuania,
None can conquer them, stay them or halt.

Пагоня

Толькі ў сэрцы трывожным пачую За краіну радзімую жах, - Ўспомню Вострую Браму святую І ваякаў на грозных канях.

Ў белай пене праносяцца коні, Рвуцца, мкнуцца і цяжка хрыпяць - Старадаўняй Літоўскай Пагоні
Не разбіць, не спыніць, не стрымаць.

У бязмерную даль вы ляціце, А за вамі, прад вамі - гады.
Вы за кім у пагоню спяшыце? Дзе шляхі вашы йдуць і куды?

Мо яны, Беларусь, панясліся За тваімі дзяцьмі ўздагон, Што забылі цябе, адракліся, Прадалі і аддалі ў палон?

Біце ў сэрцы іх - біце мячамі, Не давайце чужынцамі быць! Хай пачуюць, як сэрца начамі Аб радзімай старонцы баліць.

Маці родная, Маці-краіна! Не усцішыцца гэтакі боль…
Ты прабач, Ты прымі свайго сына, За Цябе яму ўмерці дазволь!..

Ўсё лятуць і лятуць тыя коні, Срэбнай збруяй далёка грымяць… Старадаўняй Літоўскай Пагоні
Не разбіць, не спыніць, не стрымаць.

Translated by Vera Rich

A wrinkle

The sound of emptiness
It lasts…
And lasts…
Swishing with light
And smoke whitish paste
There…
Beyond the fog,
Faces passed
With barefoot thoughts
Carried…
Without haste…

Step
By step,
Blurring middles,
A lifeline
Is wrapped
Around knitting needles
Of His…
At the end…

Being
A flowing line
So little,
I hope
To become
Not sorrowful
Wrinkle…
On His
Face.

11

DECEMBER

***

I knelt before your shadow, begging you to love me.
I didn't give a damn about my pride and dignity.
Yet it was cold eyes, not a man, that stared down scornfully.
And I turned in on myself, my heart weeping helplessly.

If you're so clever, don't show you don't love me;
My poor heart is tender and broken so easily.
Don't be sorry – or glad – you kissed my neck briefly;
A woman must be allowed to retain her dignity.

May the rain pour down like my tears from the skies.
I seem to have been shrunken by cold, cruel eyes.
Dark days are coming that rob me of happiness.
It seems I've been sent to an island of loneliness.

You disdained me as a silly woman or worse
But how's it wrong to plead for love in verse?
I have loved only one man in my life to this time.
I saw him as honourable, an angel sublime.

You're not innocent in my poetry, it's true.
Too bad my best verse wasn't written for you.
But don't you dare treat me as if I'm a fool.
I cried many tears when I lost honour's jewel.

Couldn't you indulge a child, a poet of dreams?
Just pretend you like it, however raw it seems.
I wouldn't treat you so cruelly, God of Love –
Why not join in my song: inspire me from above?

12
DECEMBER

***

Spreading my great wings out in the air
I was flying ahead of my time.
Let people who don't understand
Stare at me in amazement.

A crown is the herald of the feeling of light
That glows through all mankind.
The Almighty will never blame me
If the sun follows me into the dark.

***

Do I have to accept my lot
And fulfil the destiny
Chosen by the Lord for me
By mistake?
I don't want to suffer.
Dear Lord, have mercy on me.
Let the warm rays of the sun
Penetrate my cold bed.

***

I'll never again know the tenderness I have now.
Lightning won't flash through my dreams any more.
We should not be deceived by forlorn hopes
And stay waiting for a Good Man.

Stay away from cold, cold eyes,
Let's go to the voids of desert, water and cloud
Let's stray to the unseen, unknown, unheard world
Where my love can't go unnoticed.

I'll wrap you away and hide you in my pocket
So that people don't gossip and judge.
May all my good verses turn into waves
And let's live out on the wide ocean!

***

I always prayed that the Almighty one day
Would send me my life's one true light,
And yes, I've regrets in longing this way,
But our meeting brimmed with delight.

I never thought sweet words of joy
Would swiftly turn quite so hollow,
But now it seems I've become a mere toy
Of the deceptive romance that followed.

I wanted you to be my spirit's good healing
And not just caress my hair.
Stop here now: you're betraying my feeling –
I won't forgive you this sham love affair.

06 MONDAY

07 TUESDAY

08 WEDNESDAY

09 THURSDAY

10 FRIDAY

11 SATURDAY   12 SUNDAY

SAGYN BERKINALIEVA (KYRGYZSTAN)

***

Now we are the casualties
Of shameless lies and slurs again.
Like a venomous snake, cold words
Wind and slither down our lane.

And now I'm lying in my grave –
He buried me before I was dead.
I am so hurt by this man of ice –
The man with who I shared my bed.

Josephine, you're so receptive –
Like a mother you've been to me
You were sent by the Almighty
As my inseparable twin to be.

***

Such dangerous steps I take today –
And who will look after me?
Will I find comfort in the poppies
That in fairyland grow free?

Yet it seems even the poppies wither –
They're tumbling down the slope.
And when the sky starts falling too,
It smashes my heart's hope.

There's really no eluding
What destiny has shown.
Any sacrifice is useless
When it's written down in stone.

Every further step's a sin
Even though it's brief,
But guiltless, sinless days
Bring my heart such grief.

Let me be a girl of snow
In a fairy tale from long ago.

13

DECEMBER

***

Are you sorry you kissed my neck briefly?
And touched my hands my accidentally?
You pretended that you were drunk.
Of course, you deceived me completely.

Instead of protesting your indifference,
Smile and show more benevolence.
Shower my poems with sweet delights
Like soft rain falling from the heights.

My feelings would mount the wingéd horse
And race upon the west-wind's course,
Then spread out through the wide, wide sky,
Wrapped in their cloudy, heavenly source.

Yes, I let myself trust in the words of men
And I became an object of derision.
I so admired your cold, dark eyes then,
But I was looking for love beyond your vision.

Maybe you thought of me as a feeble soul,
Unworthy of a man's admiration.
So why did you play such a loving role
Then abandon me to denigration.

This one-way love won't drive me mad;
I won't lose my head and go insane.
I can't live without you – yes, that's bad.
But I won't beg you to caress me again.

I'll do my best to sustain my dignity.
How can the ignorant know my value?
The one true judge is the Almighty;
I'll live well with no regrets for you.

And let your applause sweetly roll.
Today, flowers bloom in my heart –
White lilies, the queens of the soul.
For you, a garden's unfurled,
And my lilies will cover the world.

Butterflies of gorgeous hues are dancing
here before my eyes,
And as I write down every verse,
it seems I am in paradise.
I have become Happiness's choir.
Look at me, people, and admire!

Applaud me, cheer me, warmly praise me –
Help my inspiration raise me.
May in my words joy be revealed.
Dear folks, let yourselves be healed!

AINUR KUMARKHANOVA (KAZAKHSTAN)

Sometimes I want to match Abai

My dreams have sailed away
The spark in me has died.
I can no longer look that way
The spirit's gone inside.

When my friend became my foe
And hit me on the brow.
The dispute that brought us low
Is a rift forever now.

People cannot be put right.
Our life's not mended by and by.
I'm not the devil here in sight
And I won't die in this lie.

I had a simple dream
To be like everyone.
To work hard at the seam
And find simple joy and fun.

You know Abai used to say
He had high hopes for his people,
But I wish I'd reached his way
And joined him on his steeple.

But people feel despair
And look for hope all round.
They go on searching everywhere
Then are sad it can't be found.

You should know your level well
As the saying goes, "Get real!"
Talking yourself up and the hard sell.
Won't help your soul or how you feel.

Your grief won't give way to freedom
You just keep it all within…

14

DECEMBER

Let`s go to our native village

For months my soul, heart and mood
Longed to go to our native village.
Then completely shaken by yearning
I got ready quickly. I couldn't imagine
My life without my childhood home any more.
Why not all go to the country,
And overcome our sadness.
We can send news to the family at once,
Early in the morning, to our little palace.
I quickly gathered my sisters –
One is overjoyed: "We're going home!"
The iron horse sped on and I whisper:
"Oh, fly racehorse - defeat homesick syndrome".
We'll read the Quran to our deceased parents
Ans we'll ask the neighbours on this occasion
About how our ancestors lived and many events.
Eyewitnesses will tell us truthfully with passion.
We'll remember our childhood pranks,
We'll share news, discuss life problems.
"The country's link to the city, say some people
Never breaks as long as there is a thread between them".
The Universe won't forget repeat to me... of course
The men of the villages are magnanimous souls
The Universe will remind; here is my source -
The beginning of my great path through life, my ground.
I go hand in hand with you, my native village
Softly as a parent who says that home is best!
Descendants, ancestors we`re of one blood, one lineage
And all my ardour cannot be held in my excited chest!

17
DECEMBER

In this first ever collection of Sakha poems in our English language, the highly talented poet Natalia Kharlampieva weaves openly neo-Impressionistic threads of common heritage, communal faith and shared ethnicity, into an overall tapestry of cultural optimism. Indeed, to Kharlampieva's mind, the unique significance played by independent women (willing to endure every hardship) in these restorative endeavours clearly signals the spiritual strength of Central Asia. A lesson, moreover, she obliquely suggests the West itself still needs to learn. Of course, in Kharlampieva's case, these powerful declamations are set against the grinding impact of icy expanses on Sakha psyches. And as such, Kharlampieva invites the readers of Foremother Asia into a hardy, but delicate world: a narratorial sphere characterised by the need to survive against all odds. Indeed, once her reader's grasp that the capital city of the Sakha Republic is located a mere 450 kilometres south of the Arctic Circle, they will begin to accept the insights of this crisp and original volume as a singular contribution to Global Text. Unanimously applauded as an impassioned book revealing the delights of a recovered national identity, Kharlampieva also captures Natures savage beauty, as well as the harsh existential truths of life in the far North.

ISBN: 978-1910886229
RRP: £17.50

13 MONDAY

14 TUESDAY

15 WEDNESDAY

16 THURSDAY

17 FRIDAY

18 SATURDAY

19 SUNDAY

BORDER BALLAD

March, march, Ettrick and Teviotdale,
Why the deil dinna ye march forward in order!
March, march, Eskdale and Liddesdale,
All the Blue Bonnets are bound for the Border.
Many a banner spread,
Flutters above your head,
Many a crest that is famous in story.
Mount and make ready then,
Sons of the mountain glen,
Fight for the Queen and our old Scottish glory.

Come from the hills where your hirsels are grazing,
Come from the glen of the buck and the roe;
Come to the crag where the beacon is blazing,
Come with the buckler, the lance, and the bow.
Trumpets are sounding,
War-steeds are bounding,
Stand to your arms, then, and march in good order;
England shall many a day
Tell of the bloody fray,
When the Blue Bonnets came over the Border.

20

DECEMBER

Пограничная баллада (RUSSIAN)

Шагайте, шагайте, Эттрик и Тевиотдейл ,
Какого черта вы не держите строй!
Шагайте, шагайте, Эггсдейл и Лидделсдейл ,
Все Синие береты направляются к Границе.
До горизонта простираются ряды Синих беретов,
Они трепещут над головами,
И многие знатные мужи идут в этих рядах.
Так что восстаньте и будьте готовы,
Сыны горных долин,
Сразиться за Королеву во славу родной Шотландии!

Спускайтесь с холмов, где пасутся ваши кони,
Приходите из долин, где олени и косули;
Приходите к скале, где светит маяк,
Несите с собой щиты, копья и луки.
Трубы трубят,
Скачут боевые кони,
Берите оружие и вставайте в строй;
Англия будет много веков
Вспоминать о том кровавом дне,
Когда Синие береты пересекли Границу.

Translated by Tatiana Vasilieva

21

DECEMBER

By the mirror. An attempt at self-portrait.

And again came the hundred-eyed night, descending on the deep-sleeping Town,
Covering the necklace of lamps with a sinister dark cherry veil.
All that happened with me is forgotten, and past things are precious, but now
Those became an unknown and a sweet melody played,

Of a sudden… And where are those words that made pale cheeks then blush,
That ignited the fire of a taciturn daring longing?
Framed in a window duvet, a blue mist of a knapweed dark rush
Lies on shoulders of mine. In its grip the cold night is now holding

Both my hands… But I listen to music again:
That small reed that now sobs, but then would drive insane and demand.
Dark-blue vaults are on shoulders of Atlases, withstanding pain.
I will nod to reflection: Margaret.

23

DECEMBER

Immortelles.
(A flower waltz of orange-coloured leaves…)

A flower waltz of orange-coloured leaves,
> that flow down to the bedhead of the forest…
A Magdalene's sweet dream that we call love,
> oh, yes, this pain that's often called affection,

As by mistake: a disaffection. It's a crystal ball, a novel's foreword to the rest…

…What did that Hopeless day predict:
> was one to be revived or to fall dead?

We fell on the hot sand, we had no strength: the shore span us around

With life's events huge dragging net.

With azure splash, with thousands words about
> eternity and freedom, being tranquil,

With willow leaves – and billions of eyes, and all the words said then instead of us,
Inheritance of soul, so witch-like and so evil,

Imprinted… And with tidings about lands,
> where there's a port of Sailings and Farewells,

Where Time is like an immortelle within me,
> a silver immortelle that sleeps inside,

And immortality that's sitting deep in me,
> that all the mystery events for me foretells

As well as future lives…

Книга «Өң мен түс» написана в жанре поэзии. Привлекает читателя особенностью стиля, многогранной содержанию слова. Автор очень рано начала свой творческий путь. В итоге достигла словесное мастерство, красочный художественный мотив, могла передать их в своем творчестве. Вышли десять сборников автора в жанре поэзии и прозы.

«Сердце матери» - так называется очередная поэма поэтессы. Это - первое поэтическое произведение написанное на небе. Излитая цепочка на 1500 строк, которая родилась в течении 2-3 часа на авиалайнере, произвела огромное впчатление читателей и создала аншлаг в аэропорту.

Сборник Шамшии Жубатовой своего рода - исповедь души, историей любви человечеству, родному краю, детям. Простата изложения сложного мировоззрения-достоинство словесного мастера. Книга является открытием Мира, совершенно нового Времени, прихода и рождения другого поколения.

Стихи вошедшие в сборник характеризуются смелостью, выразительным акцентом, скоростью мыслей.
Книга «Өң мен түс» -спокойный и тихий голос постоянно звучащий внутри каждого из нас. Нужно только научиться слушать их.

ISBN: 978-1-910886-69-4
RRP: £9.50

26

DECEMBER

20 MONDAY

21 TUESDAY

23 WEDNESDAY

24 THURSDAY

25 FRIDAY

26 SATURDAY   27 SUNDAY

Кел, балалар, оқылық!

Бір құдайға сыйынып,
Кел, балалар, оқылық,
Оқығанды көңілге
Ықыласпен тоқылық!
Істің болар қайыры,
Бастасаңыз Аллалап,
Оқымаған жүреді
Қараңғыны қармалап.
Кел, балалар, оқылық,
Оқығанды көңілге,
Ықыласпен тоқылық!

Let's Learn, Children!

Pray only to God,
And, children, get reading!
Enjoy a good book –
Mix pleasure with learning!
It would be such a shame
If you started under God's eyes
Then fell through ignorance
Into where darkness lies.
So, children, get reading!
Enjoy a good book –
Mix pleasure with learning!

27

DECEMBER

Hanba

Ja plakal som nad sudbou Sláva,
no zmĺkol plač i zmĺkol spev.
A v dlane rúk mi klesla hlava.
Žiaľ nezhynul a búri hnev
a odberá mi pokoj duši,
o rode spev môj predsa čuší.

I milujem ja jednu krásku.
Hľa, nad rodom som neplakal,
a ako k deve cítim lásku,
ju ospevujem, bôľ i žiaľ.
Ó, zmĺkni spev. Ó, zmlčte muky!
Vypadni pero z trasnej ruky!

Shame

I long wept for the glory of Fame,
But then my song and cry were hushed.
My hands covered my face in shame.
Alas, unchecked, my anger flashed
And took my peace, my soul was hurt.
My song about us still is heard.

I sang love songs and deeply sighed,
When with one girl I fell in love.
About my nation have I cried?
Now I feel pain on its behalf.
O, hush my song! O, hush my pain!
O, hand! Don't you dare write again!

29
DECEMBER

***

Ring out, wild bells, to the wild sky,
   The flying cloud, the frosty light:
   The year is dying in the night;
Ring out, wild bells, and let him die.

Ring out the old, ring in the new,
   Ring, happy bells, across the snow:
   The year is going, let him go;
Ring out the false, ring in the true.

Ring out the grief that saps the mind
   For those that here we see no more;
   Ring out the feud of rich and poor,
Ring in redress to all mankind.

Ring out a slowly dying cause,
   And ancient forms of party strife;
   Ring in the nobler modes of life,
With sweeter manners, purer laws.

Ring out the want, the care, the sin,
   The faithless coldness of the times;
   Ring out, ring out my mournful rhymes
But ring the fuller minstrel in.

Ring out false pride in place and blood,
   The civic slander and the spite;
   Ring in the love of truth and right,
Ring in the common love of good.

Ring out old shapes of foul disease;
   Ring out the narrowing lust of gold;
   Ring out the thousand wars of old,
Ring in the thousand years of peace.

Ring in the valiant man and free,
   The larger heart, the kindlier hand;
   Ring out the darkness of the land,
Ring in the Christ that is to be.

31

DECEMBER

28 MONDAY

29 TUESDAY

30 WEDNESDAY

31 THURSDAY

01 FRIDAY

02 SATURDAY   03 SUNDAY

TRANSLATORS

John Farndon: 1st January, 2nd January, 3rd April, 1st August, 28th August, 9th September, 3rd October, 12th October, 5th December

John Farndon with Alina Moseykina: 22nd January, 7th February, 14th February, 19th February, 21st February, 13th March, 22nd March, 24th March, 25th March, 3rd April, 1st May, 2nd May, 3rd May, 10th May, 13th May, 29th May, 13th June, 16th June, 20th June, 5th July, 8th July, 23rd July, 18th August, 23th August, 6th September, 12th September, 14th September, 20th September, 24th September, 1st October, 8th November, 17th November, 27th December, 29th December

John Farndon with Hamid Ismailov: 29th September

John Farndon with Lenifer Mambetova: 18th May

John Farndon with Olga Nakston: 28th February, 18th August

John Farndon with Lilia Belokonova: 10th January, 1st June

John Farndon with Altynai Toktomotova: 12th, 13th December

Alina Moseykina: 3rd January, 24th January, 26th February, 29th March, 31st March, 14th April, 23rd April, 6th June, 7th September, 6th October, 14th October, 23rd December

Alina Moseykina with Sagyn Berkinalieva: 18th September

Tatiana Vasilieva: 1st, 4th 7th March

Dorian Rottenberg: 10th August, 1st November

Diana Lewis Burgin: 31st January

Mike Munford: 9th May

Vera Rich: 28th June, 9th December

Walter Scott
Lars Arnell: 6th January
Artashes Poghosyan: 12th January
Yelena Aslanyan: 14th January
Yevgeny Bonver: 5th November
Carl Zwicker: 26th January
Antoni Edward Odyniec: 4th February
Unknown: 11th February
Michael Kunitsky: 2nd April
Auguste-Jean-Baptiste Defauconpret: 13th April
Irina Petrova; 22nd April
Rashid Yugaziev: 23rd May
Pavlo Grabovskiy: 11th June
Julius Krohn: 12th July
Alexander Dumas: 20th July
A. H. Tammsaare: 27th July
Jaroslav Vrchlický: 8th August
Tom Sibday: 5th October
Alina Moseykina: 25th October
Tatiana Vasilieva: 16th November, 21st November

MANY THANKS TO ALL THE TRANSLATORS!

CONTENTS

www.ingramcontent.com/pod-product-compliance
Lightning Source LLC
Chambersburg PA
CBHW041149300726
48981CB00003B/203